# THIS MORNING WITH GOD

## VOL. I

*a daily devotional guide for your quiet time*

Carol Adeney, general editor

**INTER-VARSITY PRESS**

Downers Grove, Illinois 60515

Sixth printing, August 1974

InterVarsity Press is the book
publishing division of Inter-Varsity
Christian Fellowship, a student
movement active on campus at
hundreds of universities, colleges and
schools of nursing. For information
about this dynamic association, write
IVCF, 233 Langdon, Madison,
WI 53703. If you're a student, four
chances out of five you'll find a local
IVCF chapter on your campus.

ISBN 0-87784-668-5
Library of Congress Catalog
Card Number: 68-28080

Printed in the United
States of America

Authors of Volume One:
Genesis—Alice Naumoff; Exodus—Yvonne Vinkemulder; Joshua—Donald
Wade; Psalms 1-27—Frank Currie; Psalms 28-29—James Sire; Hosea—Fred
Wagner; Amos—Burton Harding; Luke—Ronald Thompson/Yvonne Vinke-
mulder/Carol Adeney; Acts—Thomas Champness; Romans—Bill Weimer/
Martha Reapsome/Carol Adeney; Galatians—Charles Hummel, rev. by Paul
Byer; 1 Thessalonians—Elizabeth Thompson; 2 Thessalonians—Joanne Butts

# CONTENTS

|  | date started | date finished |
|---|---|---|
| ☐ Luke 1-9 | | |
| ☐ Genesis 1-26 | | |
| ☐ Luke 10:1-19:28 | | |
| ☐ Genesis 27-50 | | |
| ☐ Luke 19:29-24:53 | | |
| ☐ Psalms 1-12 | | |
| ☐ Acts 1-12 | | |
| ☐ Exodus 1-20 | | |
| ☐ Acts 13-28 | | |
| ☐ Amos | | |
| ☐ Hosea | | |
| ☐ Psalms 13-29 | | |
| ☐ 1 Thessalonians | | |
| ☐ 2 Thessalonians | | |
| ☐ Joshua | | |
| ☐ Galatians | | |
| ☐ Exodus 21-40 | | |
| ☐ Romans | | |

| BOOK | VOLUME | 1 | 2 | 3 | 4 |
|---|---|---|---|---|---|
| Genesis | | ■ | | | |
| Exodus | | ■ | | | |
| Leviticus | | | ■ | | |
| Numbers | | | ■ | | |
| Deuteronomy | | | ■ | | |
| Joshua | | ■ | | | |
| Judges | | | ■ | | |
| Ruth | | | | ■ | |
| 1 Samuel | | | ■ | | |
| 2 Samuel | | | | ■ | |
| 1 Kings | | | | ■ | |
| 2 Kings | | | | ■ | |
| 1 Chronicles | | | | | ■ |
| 2 Chronicles | | | | | ■ |
| Ezra | | | | | ■ |
| Nehemiah | | | | | ■ |
| Esther | | | | | ■ |
| Job | | | | ■ | |
| Psalms 1-29 | | ■ | | | |
| 30-41 | | | ■ | | |
| 42-72 | | | | ■ | |
| 73-150 | | | | | ■ |
| Proverbs | | | ■ | | |
| Ecclesiastes | | | | | ■ |
| Song of Solomon | | | | | ■ |
| Isaiah | | | | ■ | |
| Jeremiah | | | | | ■ |
| Lamentations | | | | | ■ |
| Ezekiel | | | | | ■ |
| Daniel | | | | | ■ |
| Hosea | | ■ | | | |
| Joel | | | | ■ | |
| Amos | | ■ | | | |
| Obadiah | | | | ■ | |

| BOOK | VOLUME | 1 | 2 | 3 | 4 |
|---|---|---|---|---|---|
| Jonah | | | | ■ | |
| Micah | | | ■ | | |
| Nahum | | | | ■ | |
| Habakkuk | | | | ■ | |
| Zephaniah | | | | ■ | |
| Haggai | | | | | ■ |
| Zechariah | | | | | ■ |
| Malachi | | | | | ■ |
| Matthew | | | | | ■ |
| Mark | | | ■ | | |
| Luke | | ■ | | | |
| John | | | | ■ | |
| Acts | | ■ | | | |
| Romans | | ■ | | | |
| 1 Corinthians | | | ■ | | |
| 2 Corinthians | | | ■ | | |
| Galatians | | ■ | | | |
| Ephesians | | | | ■ | |
| Philippians | | | | ■ | |
| Colossians | | | | ■ | |
| 1 Thessalonians | | ■ | | | |
| 2 Thessalonians | | ■ | | | |
| 1 Timothy | | | ■ | | |
| 2 Timothy | | | ■ | | |
| Titus | | | ■ | | |
| Philemon | | | | ■ | |
| Hebrews | | | ■ | | |
| James | | | | | ■ |
| 1 Peter | | | ■ | | |
| 2 Peter | | | | | ■ |
| 1 John | | | | ■ | |
| 2 John | | | | ■ | |
| 3 John | | | | ■ | |
| Jude | | | | | ■ |
| Revelation | | | | | ■ |

## BEFORE YOU START

The Bible is the book about God and his relationship to all men. That the infinite God of the universe desires to relate himself to people is probably the most awesome fact of history. The Bible records the thoughts and experiences of rulers, poets, housewives, doctors, prophets, carpenters, students, business men . . . as they lived and learned to understand God's relationship to them.

But the Bible is not only about other people; it is about you too. You will find your own mental, emotional, social struggles in its pages. As you read the Bible, God's words will focus upon your contemporary situation. They will show you how and why God wants to relate to you. The Bible can change your life.

# ABOUT *this morning with God*

## WHAT?

*This morning with God* is a guide to help you discover what the Bible says and means to you. By following this plan, you can study the entire Bible in five years. Each book of the Bible is divided into a number of daily studies which cover several paragraphs of the book.

Each daily study contains several get-at-the-meaning questions. You will find that the questions are of three basic types: to help you observe (What does the text say?), interpret (What does it mean?), and apply (What does it mean *to you*). These different questions are balanced to help keep your study from becoming *only* objective or *only* subjective. They have been chosen to focus on the main ideas in your daily reading.

The questions are based on the *Revised Standard Version* of the Bible because of its paragraph divisions and its up-to-date language. Supplementary comparison with other translations can often explain and simplify difficult passages.

## WHO?

*This morning with God* is for anyone who wants to know how the Bible affects and transforms life. It assumes that you are serious about the Bible's content, not *only* interested in its historical or literary merits.

If you have never read the Bible before, *this morning with God* can help you grasp the main ideas. If you know a lot *about* the Bible, but have little first-hand discovery, *this morning with God* can guide you as you dig out the truth for yourself. If you have never stuck to a plan of Bible reading before, *this morning with God* can stimulate you to digest bite-sized readings with down-to-earth questions. If you want a fresh guide to spark and vitalize your Bible reading, *this morning with God* can be that "shot in the arm." Students, businessmen, housewives, Sunday school teachers, secretaries, farmers, nurses . . . *this morning with God* is for you.

## WHY?

*This morning with God* is a guide for *inductive* study of the Bible. It asks questions to help you discover what the passages mean. It does not contain outlines, historical notes, opinions, commentary, inspirational thoughts. *This morning with God* focuses on the text of the Bible—to let the Bible speak for itself.

This inductive method does not predetermine nor prejudice your investigation; it enables you to come to your own conclusions. It does not spoon feed you; it allows you the joy of independent discovery. It does not give you ready-made answers; it acquaints you with primary source material to test the validity of answers. It is not the ultimate; it aims to help you establish good inductive study methods.

Because *this morning with God* is not a study by themes, but book-by-book, it contains few topical cross-references. It respects the author's time of writing and source material. Books which directly relate to one another are grouped for your own comparison. For example, because Moses did not refer to *Hebrews* since it was not written then, the study of Moses' books does not contain cross-references to *Hebrews*. But because the author of *Hebrews* had access to Moses' writings, appropriate cross-references are included in *Hebrews*. Also, Moses' books and *Hebrews* are grouped so that the background books are studied first.

The study order aims for variety among the long and short books, Old and New Testaments, and various book types. Since many people have written and revised the questions of a book, you will find different styles and emphases.

## WHEN?

*This morning with God* is designed especially for use during your Quiet Time. The daily studies, which require about twenty minutes, are grouped in 30-day sequences so that you may start the plan at the beginning of any month. Use the extra days in 31-day months for review and evaluation.

You will probably find that forming a time-habit will help you "keep at it." But your schedule of a definite 20-minute uninterrupted period every day may need to be flexible enough for unexpected events. You may also want to allow extra time during the week for catching up or for further study.

## WHERE?

*This morning with God* is for you to use anywhere—student union, kitchen, library, commuter train. Wherever you can concentrate well is an appropriate place for *this morning with God* and you.

## HOW?

*This morning with God* is only a means to an end. The end is knowing and enjoying God and his relationship with you. A specific means can not guarantee an end, but these suggestions may help make your study time more effective.

1/ EXPECT TO LEARN SOMETHING DEFINITE
You have, no doubt, found that your attitude at the beginning of any reading or study is very important. When you expect to learn nothing, your preparation and reading tend to be haphazard. But when you expect to learn something, you prepare and read *actively*. You don't sit back and hope for some magic osmosis; you become *involved* with what you are reading.

*Active preparation* should include concentration and prayer. Ask the Holy Spirit to guide as you pray, read, interpret, and apply. Ask him to overcome any "blocks" due to your mood, attitude, or distractions and to show you what you should learn in your present situation.

*Active reading* should include alertness and a method of study. Watch for important clues to the context, content, meaning, and purpose of the book; use a dictionary; organize what you find in whatever way most benefits you. The daily questions are meant to help organize your observation, interpretation, and application. You may also want to jot down questions and notes of your own.

2/ WRITE DOWN WHAT YOU LEARN Writing is an important part of understanding. It helps clarify and organize your thinking. Write down specific ideas, principles, applications, resolutions. Summary sentences, outlines, charts, poetry, and paraphrases may be useful. You may also want to list questions and problems for further study.

3/ ACT OUT WHAT YOU LEARN  You can test your understanding of what you learn by examining the results in your life. When your thoughts, attitudes, and actions remain the same, your understanding is superficial. You may want to write out specific resolutions, review them periodically, and evaluate the results. Ask the Holy Spirit to make what you learn a part of your life in the classroom, office, kitchen, dorm, ballpark, cornfield, hospital, church, and restaurant.

Historic note: *this morning with God* studies originally appeared in HIS magazine, monthly publication of Inter-Varsity Christian Fellowship, prior to 1960. These studies are revised and adapted for continuous use.

# ABOUT SUPPLEMENTARY HELPS

In addition to your Bible, *this morning with God,* a dictionary, and notebooks, you may also want to use some of these supplementary helps (but read the Bible first):

*Oxford Concise Concordance*° (rsv)— an alphabetical list of biblical words with their parallel passages

*The New Bible Handbook*°— background information on every book of the Bible and articles on inspiration, authority, the canon, modern criticism, history, geography, and biblical content

*The New Bible Commentary*°— extensive comments and explanation of biblical passages, paragraph-by-paragraph

*The New Bible Dictionary*°— definitions and explanations of biblical names, places, objects, concepts, customs, language, categories

a Bible atlas— location and background of biblical places

°available from Inter-Varsity Press, Box F, Downers Grove, Ill. 60515

## MONTH 1

DAY *1* ⚶ *Introduction to Luke*
Luke is an educated Gentile — physician, historian, and traveler —
concerned with the logical and historical development of the gospel
Jesus proclaims. He shows that the kingdom of God is not con-
tained in the boundaries set by Jewish religious leaders. The good
news of the gospel is also to poor, sick, outcasts, women, children,
foreigners. *Luke 1:1-25* 1/ What does Luke's own introduction
reveal about his reliability, source material, purpose, and distinction? 2/ Characterize Zechariah and Elizabeth (note their ancestry). What is Zechariah's occupation (cf. Ex. 30:7-8; 1 Chron.
24:1-10, 19)? 3/ Imagine their feelings toward Elizabeth's barrenness (if they have no children, they can't be ancestors of the
coming Messiah). 4/ Describe the situation when the angel appears. 5/ What is Zechariah's immediate reaction? 6/ Characterize John as to *a*—reaction to his birth, *b*—his relationship to God,
and *c*—his ministry. 7/ Imagine how Zechariah feels when these

12

predictions are made about his future child. Why does he look for proof? What is the angel's reply? 8/ In what ways have you questioned God's message to you? When? How has God confirmed his message? 9/ Imagine the people's feelings. How do you respond to God's work in other people? 10/ What is Elizabeth's attitude toward this coming event?

DAY 2 △ *Luke 1:26-38*

1/ Compare and contrast God's announcements to Zechariah and Mary as to *a*—salutation, *b*—basis of selection, and *c*—reaction to the message. 2/ In what ways are Elizabeth's and Mary's situation similar and different? 3/ What does the angel reveal about the identity and destiny of Jesus? 4/ What makes this birth impossible? possible? unique? What illustration is given to Mary? 5/ Contrast Mary's immediate and secondary responses. 6/ Imagine her mixed emotions (cf. Deut. 22:13-21). 7/ In what situations have you chosen between the approval of others or submission to God with a resulting stigma? What choice have you made? Why?

DAY 3 △ *Luke 1:39-56*

1/ Imagine this meeting. 2/ Describe Elizabeth's reception of Mary. How does she know Mary's "secret"? What attitude does she have toward Mary? 3/ What does Mary say concerning *a*—the character of God, *b*—his actions and activity, and *c*—his attitude toward people? On what basis does he "show partiality" (vv. 48-50, 52)? 4/ What reason does Mary give for this mighty act? 5/ Characterize these two women. 6/ In what ways is Mary personally aware of God's attributes? 7/ For which of God's attributes can you praise him today? 8/ How can you view immediate problems in the perspective of past and future history as Mary does?

DAY 4 △ *Luke 1:57-80*

1/ What controversy arises after Elizabeth gives birth? How is it stopped? 2/ How is tradition sometimes a test to your obedience? 3/ At what point is Zechariah's speech restored? 4/ If you were unable to talk for nine months or more, what would be your first words? 5/ How do the people react? In light of Zechariah's occupation account for the spread of and interest in the news. 6/ Divide Zechariah's prophecy into general and specific information. To whom does the first part refer (cf. vv. 68-69 with v. 27)? 7/ What does he say about *a*—the coming and purpose of the Messiah, *b*—the purpose of his own son, and *c*—the character and actions of God? 8/ What is the purpose of deliverance (vv. 74-75)? Relate *salvation* (v. 77) to this purpose and further mission (v. 79). 9/ How have you experienced this full deliverance? 10/ Measure the purpose of your life with verses 73-75 and 79. 11/ What is significant about both Zechariah's and Mary's referring to the broad sweep of history? 12/ Describe John's youth.

### DAY 5   △   *Luke 2:1-20*

1/ Imagine yourself in the place of these people. What are your feelings? 2/ Trace the trip of Joseph and Mary on a map. From the divine perspective why is the trip necessary (cf. Micah 5:2)? 3/ Imagine the hardship of the trip for Mary's physical condition. 4/ Describe the conditions surrounding the birth. 5/ How much hardship, frustration, and inconvenience are you willing to endure as God's instrument? 6/ To whom and under what circumstances is the first birth announcement made? What vital statistics are given about the baby? 7/ Imagine the shepherds' feelings as they tend to business. Visualize the night interruption. What is the shepherds' initial reaction? 8/ In what ways do you limit the time and place of God's message to you? Do you listen to him as you go about your daily work (cf. 2:8 with 1:8ff.)? 9/ What do the shepherds do after the concert? 10/ Compare the responses of *a*—the shepherds, *b*—those who hear the spreading news, and *c*—Mary. 11/ What are the three phases of the shepherds' response? In what ways does their response parallel your experience?

### DAY 6   △   *Luke 2:21-39*

1/ How do Joseph and Mary comply with God's demands (cf. Gen. 17:9-13; Ex. 13:2, 13; Lev. 12)? 2/ What does verse 24 reveal about their economic situation (cf. Lev. 12:8)? 3/ In what ways does the birth, parentage, etc. of Jesus differ from your expectations of the birth of a king (cf. 1:32-33)? 4/ Characterize Simeon. What is he doing in the temple (v. 27)? 5/ How does he view the new baby? How does he have this insight? What does he prophesy about Jesus? What does he foresee for Mary? 6/ In what way does Simeon have revelation beyond that given to Zechariah (cf. vv. 31-32 with 1:77)? 7/ Imagine yourself in the place of Joseph and Mary doing what is required after the birth of a child. What is your reaction to all of this? Compare or contrast Joseph and Mary's reaction with your imagined one. 8/ Characterize Anna. What is her evaluation and response to the child? 9/ In a society dominated by tradition under pagan government what is significant about the people described in these chapters? 10/ Compare this situation to church and national life today. 11/ Can you characterize yourself as *righteous and devout?* On what basis?

### DAY 7  △  *Luke 2:40-52*

1/ What additional insight do verses 41-42 reveal about Jesus' home (cf. Ex. 13:3-10) and his parents' attitude toward God (cf. v. 39)? 2/ Depict the situon on the way home. 3/ What has this twelve-year-old been doing for probably five days? What is so astonishing about this? What is the teachers' response? 4/ With what are you occupied when not involved in the daily routine of life? 5/ What are Jesus' views of a—his identity, b—his parents' anxiety? 6/ Have you ever felt that you are not fully understood by your parents or family? Imagine how Jesus feels in this situation. 7/ What is his relationship with Joseph and his attitude toward parental authority (vv. 49-51)? 8/ What is your attitude toward authority? 9/ Compare verse 51 with verses 19 and 33 to see how Mary handles information which she can't understand. 10/ From verses 40 and 52 describe Jesus' childhood. Are you growing in similar directions?

### DAY 8  △  *Luke 3:1-20*

1/ Establish the religious and political setting as John begins his preaching. Locate on a map and identify the historical cross-references. 2/ How do these references support the trustworthiness of the record? 3/ What is John's purpose (messengers are customarily sent to warn and exhort people to get ready for a royal visit—relate John's purpose to the times)? his message? his authority? 4/ How does he approach the people? 5/ Characterize *vipers*. How is this metaphor apt? 6/ How is John's message a fulfillment of Isaiah's prophecy? 7/ Relate his message to road building (vv.

4-5), wood cutting (v. 9), and harvesting (v. 17). 8/ What is
*a*—God's and *b*—man's part in these actions? 9/ What are the practical outreaches of true repentance? What is the effect of obedience
personally? to others? 10/ In what ways do you bear *fruits of
repentance?* What effect does this have on others? What can you do
today? 11/ What misconception does John clear up? What is
John's self-concept when compared to Christ? 12/ In what way
is his message *good news?* How are exhortations *good news?* 13/
Contrast the responses to his preaching. 14/ What is your reaction
when your sin and injustice is exposed? What is *good news* about
that? 15/ What stands out about John's character?

DAY 9  △  *Luke 3:21-38*
1/ Why is John baptizing (v. 3)? 2/ Contrast this with the reason Jesus is baptized (cf. Mt. 3:13-15). How does Jesus' baptism
show the extent he identifies with man? 3/ In what two ways is
Jesus' divine identity shown? 4/ What is said about his *a*—identity,
*b*—origin, and *c*—character? 5/ When does Jesus start his public
ministry? 6/ What preparation have you given to your "ministry"?
Do you often get impatient? 7/ Skim Jesus' genealogy of human
descent. What is his royal lineage (cf. v. 32 with 1:32, 69)? his
religious ancestry (cf. v. 34 with 1:55)? 8/ Why does Jesus as
both divine and human have significance for you? 9/ What is your
response to one with such an endorsement?

DAY 10  △  *Luke 4:1-15*
1/ Describe this wilderness experience of Jesus. 2/ In what ways
is he susceptible to Satan's attacks? 3/At what times are you most
susceptible to Satan's attacks? 4/ Compare the three tests Satan
puts to Jesus as to *a*—specific content, *b*—appeal to what aspect of
human nature, *c*—progression in intensity, and *d*—Jesus' reply. 5/
What is the real issue of the first temptation? 6/ How does the
second test clarify your understanding of the problem of evil and
world affairs (cf. vv. 6-7 with 1:32-33)? 7/ To whom does ultimate rule rightfully belong? 8/ Explain how Jesus' answer to the
third test is a fitting response to Satan's challenge. 9/ Do you
recognize temptation for what it is? 10/ Are the issues here still
temptations to the Christian church? 11/How are these temptations inconclusive? 12/ Of what value to you is knowing that

16

Jesus has been tempted in every way you are? 13/ Describe his return to Galilee. Imagine Satan's reaction to these facts.

DAY *11* △ *Luke 4:16-30*

1/ What habit does Jesus have? 2/ According to Isaiah's prophecy what is the commission and power of the messenger? Describe each of these as spiritual benefits. 3/ What does Jesus claim about himself? 4/ What is his attitude toward the scriptures? 5/ With what situations in Isaiah's prophecy do you identify? 6/ In what ways have you been *released*? been given 20—20 spiritual vision? found *liberty*? 7/ Why does Jesus refuse to perform miracles in Nazareth? 8/ What two illustrations does he use to prove his point? 9/ Contrast the reaction to his reading of scripture (vv. 20-22) and his application of it (vv. 28-30). 10/ When do you react similarly? 11/ Since Satan fails to defeat Christ (v. 13), trace throughout Luke how he attempts to destroy him and the potency of his message. 12/ How does this enlarge your understanding of Satan's tactics and your ability to cope with life?

DAY *12* △ *Luke 4:31-44*

1/ What impression does Jesus make on the people in the synagogue? 2/ What two things produce this impression? 3/ Where and under what circumstances does Luke's first recorded miracle occur? 4/ What duel identity does the demon-possessed man recognize? 5/ Contrast his expectation of Jesus' action with what Jesus does. 6/ How does this miracle support Jesus' teachings? 7/ To comprehend the next miracle consider the effect of severe illness with high fever on the human body and the need for recuperation. How complete is her healing? 8/ How does Jesus' day end? 9/ What is distinctive about the healing of demon-possessed people? 10/ Why does Jesus rebuke the demons? 11/ How does demon possession differ from common forms of insanity? 12/ How does Jesus' understanding of his purpose affect his activities and relationships? 13/ What is your purpose or goal? In what ways does this affect your activities and relationships?

DAY *13* △ *Luke 5:1-11*

1/ Visualize this beach scene. 2/ Why are the people here? 3/ What is the advantage of speaking from the boat? 4/ Imagine your response to a stranger asking to borrow your equipment and have you chauffer him.  5/ What command does Jesus give?  6/ Describe Peter's response to interference with his fishing business.  7/ What crisis does obedience to Jesus bring? What does Peter do about it?  8/ When faced with a responsibility beyond your capabilities, what do you do?  9/ Imagine the scene as the boats pull to shore. Mentally listen to the spectators' exclamations.  10/ What two alternatives seem to be possible for Peter?  11/ Imagine yourself as Peter telling your wife what has happened and why you are going to change your job.  12/ What is your response to the mighty acts of God: a-to push him out because you feel uncomfortable, b-to take him into business so you will be more successful, or c-to leave all and follow him?

DAY *14*  △  *Luke 5:12-26*

1/ What social and psychological problems result from the physical problem of leprosy (cf. Lev. 13:45-46)?  2/ Imagine how life will be changed by Jesus' words and act.  3/ How does the leper evidence faith? What does he doubt? How does Jesus dispel it?  4/ What is the first requirement of the law (cf. v. 14 with Lev. 14)? What does this reveal about Jesus' attitude toward the law?  5/ What happens as a result? How does Jesus meet this?  6/ What do you do when the pressures mount?  7/ What disturbance arises in the house?  8/ What kind of controversy does Jesus trigger? Of what is he accused? Why?  9/ How does he support his claim to forgive sin?  10/ Give three evidences of Jesus' deity from this miracle.  11/ What are three responses?  12/ On what basis are the leper and paralyzed man healed?  13/ When have you inconvenienced yourself to bring a helpless person to Christ?

DAY *15*  △  *Luke 5:27—6:11*

1/ List three complaints which the Pharisees lodge against Jesus. Give the setting for each and the incident which triggers each.  2/ How do Jesus' answers reveal the principles on which he acts?  3/ Are you as consistent in words and action?  4/ What is the point of the two parables?  5/ To what kind of men can the *new* be entrusted?  6/ Can the *new* be combined with the *old*? What will be the reaction of those who are accustomed to the *old* when they hear the *new*?  7/ What people or institutions that you know try to adapt Christian principles to their own religious systems? What is the result?  8/ What "patches" have you tried to put on your life to disguise rips, cover holes, stop leaks? What has been the result? 9/ Distinguish originality and freshness from disrespect for heritage. 10/ What are you doing to develop a *taste for new wine?*  11/ What do the Pharisees object to in verses 1-2?  12/ What is Jesus' reply to this?  13/ Do you allow the Son of man to control your life or do you bind yourself and others by your tradition?  14/ How can you express understanding and mercy within the limits God has established?  15/ How does Jesus call the bluff of the Pharisees in the last incident? What reaction does this bring?  16/ Are you saving or destroying life—doing good or doing nothing? Be specific.

*Sept.*

DAY *16*  △  *Luke 6:12-38*

1/ How does Jesus reveal his sense of responsibility when he has to choose apostles to take future leadership?  2/ What principle can you learn from his actions to apply to electing officers for your Christian group?  3/ Describe Jesus' popularity and power.  4/ Describe the present condition of those *a*-who are *blessed* and *b*-who are lamentable. Why? Contrast the present and future condition of each.  5/ Imagine the disciples' feelings about such statements.  6/ Do you feel blessed when you weep and woeful when men speak well of you?  7/ What specific actions are commanded? What is the basic principle of these actions?  8/ What are the marked differences between sinners and believers? Distinguish their motives.  9/ How are these commandments related to God's motives and actions?  10/ How can you be kind to ungrateful and selfish people today?  11/ How will the *a*-negative and *b*-positive commands in verses 37-38 fulfill the previous commands?  12/ What in your present attitudes and daily living will you change as a result of what you have learned here?

DAY *17*  △  *Luke 6:39-49*

1/ What is required in your life before you can help others? Do you have to be free from faults?  2/ How does Jesus illustrate the principles of verses 39-42?  3/ What is the cause and effect relationship in nature? in man?  4/ What do your actions reveal about you?   5/ What is the essential difference between the two men (and their metaphors)?   6/ With which do you identify now? 7/ Contrast their futures.   8/ Summarize Jesus' a-standards and b-authority in this teaching.   9/ Imagine the response of the people. What is your response?

DAY 18   △   *Luke 7:1-17*

1/ What does the centurion recognize in Jesus? How does he explain this to Jesus?   2/ Contrast the centurion's estimate of himself with a-his estimate of Jesus, b-the Jews' estimate of him, and c-Jesus' estimate of him.   3/ Does his faith or Jesus' healing rest in the worthiness attributed to him by others?   4/ How does your faith in Jesus affect the lives of others dear to you?   5/ Imagine yourself a member of the funeral procession. Visualize the happenings as you meet the great procession Jesus is leading.   6/ What extraordinary power does Jesus display?   7/ What qualities of Jesus are revealed by his actions toward the mother and son?   8/ How do the people respond to his actions? Imagine the feelings of the mother, son, and mourners.   9/ Imagine yourself one of the people who spread the report. What do you tell others? How do you answer the inevitable question, *How did he do it?*

DAY 19   △   *Luke 7:18-35*

1/ Imagine John's perplexity (cf. his message in 3:7-20).   2/ How does Jesus answer John's inquiry (cf. Isa. 35:5-6; 61:1)?   3/ What is Jesus' attitude toward him? How does Jesus characterize John (cf. Mal. 3:1)?   4/ What is Jesus' attitude toward the poor? Contrast this with the political, social, and religious opinion of the time. 5/ Contrast the response of a-the people and b-the Jewish leaders to the preaching of John.   6/ Contrast the methods of John and Jesus.   7/ How are the Jewish leaders like children in their reaction to John and Jesus?   8/ Imagine how contemporary religious leaders would have responded to John's and Jesus' preaching.   9/ What does verse 30 reveal about the seriousness of rejecting a true message because you don't like the method?   10/ How can you honor (*justify*) real wisdom today?

DAY 20   △   *Luke 7:36-50*

1/ How does this scene reveal that Jesus' ministry in not one-sided?

2/ Visualize the scene.   3/ Describe the woman's frame of mind
with at least four adjectives (people—but not usually notorious sinners—come uninvited into dining rooms and sit around the walls; for
a Jewish woman to let down her hair in public is a disgrace; kissing
the feet of a teacher is a sign of deep respect).   4/ What is Simon's
attitude toward a-himself, b-Jesus, and c-the woman? With what
criterion does Simon judge Jesus (v.39)?   5/ How does Jesus
reveal his knowledge of Simon and the woman?   6/ What does he
rebuke in Simon?   7/ In. what three ways does Jesus compare
Simon with the woman?   8/ Imagine a-Simon's, b-the woman's,
and c-the others' feelings.   9/ How does Jesus commend her love
but make clear that her love has not saved her?   10/ What is the
extent of her forgiveness? What are its results to herself? to others?
11/ Compare or contrast Jesus' attitudes and actions in this incident
with your attitudes and actions to sinners. How do you feel around
social sinners?   12/ What is the basis for your love of Jesus? To
what extent?

DAY 21   △   Luke 8:1-21

1/ Imagine you are a disciple who has left a lucrative fishing
business to preach. How do you look on this means of support (vv.
1-3)?   2/ What is the purpose of a parable?   3/ Distinguish this
type of teaching from Jesus' teaching of 6:17-49.   4/ Why, do
you think, does Jesus use examples from the ordinary life of the
people? Compare and contrast his methods with the methods of
contemporary teachers, religious leaders, and philosophers.   5/
Distinguish the four places where seeds fall and their counterparts
in man.   6/ How is the word of God like seed?   7/ Are you
responsible for how you receive the seed?   8/ Contrast the results
of the different ways of hearing Jesus' words.   9/ How could the
disciples respond to their "secret knowledge"? How are they to
respond?   10/ Since hearing the truth is not the key to spiritual
understanding, what is?   11/ How can you have more insight into
the truths of God's word?   12/ According to his teaching how are
you related to Jesus?

DAY 22   △   Luke 8:22-39

1/ Over what realms does Jesus show authority (unexpected,

violent storms are common on Galilee)? Imagine Satan's feelings as the storm intensifies.   2/ Relate Jesus' question to the disciples with their attitudes a-before and b-after the miracle.   3/ Characterize the man before and after his encounter with Jesus.   4/ What significant facts are revealed in a-the attitude of the demons toward Jesus and b-their requests of him?   5/ How do Jesus and Satan show the supreme value they place on one man?   6/ What about their concern do the people reveal by their response to Jesus' healing?   7/ How does Jesus' command to this Gentile take into account his previous state of personality and his previous reputation? 8/ How can you *declare* at home what God is doing for you?   9/ How is your faith in Jesus eliminating fear of circumstances, others, and Satan in practical ways? In what specific situations?

DAY 23   △   *Luke 8:40-56*
1/ What is the attitude of this ruler of the Jews toward Jesus in the beginning?   2/ Imagine Jairus' feelings at a-the interruption and b-the further news.   3/ In what ways may the incident with the woman have strengthened his faith in Jesus?   4/ Considering her problem (cf. Lev. 15:23-30) imagine the woman's state of mind. 5/ How does Jesus make clear to her what has made her well (contrast with her initial action)?   6/ How do you know that Jesus' healing is not magic (cf. v. 46)?   7/ Is Jesus' healing power dependent on man's faith?   How are his miracles and man's faith related?   8/ What qualities of Jesus are revealed by his attitudes and actions in this passage?   9/ How does Jesus' command to the parents differ from his command to the man of the Gerasenes? Why, do you think?   10/ How does the Lord's knowledge of situations strengthen your faith in his specific commands to you? Can you be trusted to be silent as well as to speak?

DAY 24   △   *Luke 9:1-17*
1/ What is the twofold ministry of the twelve?   2/ What is the source of their power and authority?   3/ How does this endowment insure the continuance of Jesus' works after his death?   4/ Compare and contrast this power and continuance with later and contemporary movements.   5/ How are the twelve supported (pagan priests carry *bags* for money they receive from begging)?   6/ What

attitudes are required to follow Jesus' instructions? 7/ Imagine the people's feelings as the disciples act in accordance with verse 5. 8/ What impresses Herod? 9/ What situations of leadership training does Jesus put the disciples through (vv. 1-2, 10, 13)? 10/ What leadership principles can you learn from this section? 11/ What part does man's physical need have in the ministry of Jesus and his disciples? 12/ What is your attitude toward meeting people's physical needs? 13/ Work out the account of verses 12-17 in columns of a-demand and b-available supply. 14/ List the areas in your life where the demands seem much greater than your supply. What help do you find here?

DAY 25  △  *Luke 9:18-36*

1/ What are various opinions of Jesus' identity? 2/ How does Peter's understanding differ from the other opinions? 3/ How have Jesus' past teaching and actions contributed to the disciples' understanding of his identity? 4/ Why, do you think, does Jesus choose this time to announce his future? What do the Jews expect about the Messiah? 5/ List and explain the requirements of one who wishes to follow *the Christ of God*. 6/ What additional meaning does *follow me* have after verse 22? 7/ In what ways will you *deny* yourself and *follow* Jesus today? 8/ What happens as Jesus prays (cf. other situations in 3:21; 6:12; 9:18)? 9/ Describe Jesus' appearance (cf. v. 26). Define *glory*. 10/ What is the meaning of the transfiguration to Jesus? to Peter, John, and James? What is the purpose of Moses and Elijah? of God's voice? 11/ What suggestion does Peter make? What does he misunderstand? 12/ How, do you think, does he recognize Moses and Elijah? 13/ Imagine the effect of this incident on the development of the three disciples' understanding and character. 14/ In what ways has God recently enlarged your understanding of him? How has this understanding been revealed in your character?

DAY 26  △  *Luke 9:37-62*

1/ What do the disciples know about Jesus (v. 20)? 2/ What do they expect from him after verse 27? 3/ What may they have concluded from the experiences of verses 28-32 and 43? 4/ How does the statement of Jesus in verse 44 contrast with their expectations? 5/ What is the result in their understanding? 6/ What kind of attitude do the disciples have in verses 40, 46, 49-50, 54-56? How does Jesus deal with their attitude?   7/ What do the disciples misunderstand about the kingdom of God? . 8/ Contrast *a*-the disciples' (v. 46) and Jesus' concern (v. 44) and *b*-the disciples' and Jesus' concept of greatness.   9/ Imagine the bitterness of the Jewish-Samaritan feud (cf. Ezra 4:1-5; Neh. 2:20).   10/ What is *a*-Jesus' and *b*-your attitude toward other Christian groups? Toward people who are hostile toward him?   11/ In what practical ways does individual and group pride distort what you and others know of God?   12/ How does Jesus respond to the three people who want to follow him?   13/ Do you use the same principles in your witness?   14/ Briefly summarize what you have learned so far from *Luke* about *a*-God, *b*-Jesus, *c*-Satan, *d*-the disciples, *e*-the religious leaders, *f*-the masses, and *g*-you.

DAY 27   △   *Introduction to Genesis*

*Genesis* introduces every theme and problem discussed in scripture. *Genesis* is the key to God's eternal plan and purpose in creation and to man's fall and increasingly deeper estrangement from God, himself, and others. And it is above all a record of God's continuous reconciling actions both in and through individuals and the Jewish nation. *Genesis 1*   1/ Given a formless void, how would you have created the universe differently (note that *create* does not mean *refashion*)?   2/ How, do you think, are God's imagination and his words related?   3/ How is man in God's image? How does he differ in kind, not merely in degree, from other creatures?   4/ What difference does this fact make in your daily life, especially in your relations with others?   5/ What in the story of creation shows not only God's greatness but also his goodness?   6/ How do you show God's concern for nature in your treatment of wildlife and natural resources?

DAY 28   △   *Genesis 2*

1/ What seems to be God's view of the "natural"? What are your views?   2/ Describe man's setting. Why, do you think, does God give man work to do before his fall?   3/ How are you approaching today's manual and mental tasks?   4/ Does God create evil (*i.e.*, the experiential knowledge of it)? Give reason for his allowing such a possibility here.   5/ How do you know that God is interested in your loneliness? What difference, practically, does knowing God make in this area?

### DAY 29  △  *Genesis 3*

1/ Characterize the serpent.   2/ How does Eve fall? What is the progression?   3/ How do you respond or react to what God says? Why?   4/ What are Adam and Eve's responses to God's sound? How are their responses the normal reaction of all men?   5/ What difference does this knowledge make in how you witness?   6/ What are their responses to a discovered sin?   7/ What do you blame your sins and problems on?   8/ What is significant about God's words to the serpent, Adam, and Eve?   9/ How is the attitude toward work changed?   10/ What do you learn here about God's character for which to praise him?

### DAY 30  △  *Genesis 4*

1/ How do you *know* God (the Jewish idea of *knowing* is not mere intellectual apprehension of a fact but experiential, intimate, active, existential knowledge)? To what extent?   2/ What is Cain's problem?   3/ In what ways does Cain disclaim responsibility for his actions? What are the results of his actions?   4/ Who is responsible for your actions?   5/ What happens to man and his environment to make him suddenly *call upon the name of the Lord*?   6/ Compare this and today's situation. Would these people call on God for anything different today?

## MONTH 2

### DAY 1  △  *Genesis 5*

1/ Suppose there were more than two sexes. What if God had left this matter to "natural selection"?   2/ Apart from difficulties in transmitting and translating Hebrew numbers, why, do you think, do people seem to live longer here?   3/ What does to *walk with God* mean? How are you *walking with God* today?

### DAY 2  △  *Genesis 6*

1/ How are the moral and physical world related?   2/ In what ways is the *earth* corrupt? What does this show about God?   3/ How does this state of man, including those you expect to be godly, compare with man today?   4/ Do you think God is "sorry" that he has made you?   5/ In the long time of building the ark what reservations, fears, doubts, and problems may have beset Noah? 6/ How do you respond to "incredible, strange, and unpopular" instructions from God?

### DAY 3   △   *Genesis 7*

1/ Characterize Noah.   2/ What happens to him? to the earth? 3/ Imagine Noah's situation with all those animals.   4/ While you are protected by God, what job has he given you to do today?   5/ How do man's sins affect the natural environment? What are you doing to lessen these effects?

### DAY 4   △   *Genesis 8*

1/ Imagine Noah's feelings after such a catastrophy.   2/ What are your feelings when tragedy happens to those who reject God?   3/ How does Noah respond to God's deliverance?   4/ What has God done for you recently? How have you responded?   5/ What is God's view of man   6/ What makes man a sinner—what he does or what he is? How does this fact make a crucial difference in your attitude toward yourself and others?

### DAY 5   △   *Genesis 9*

1/ What is God's view of human life? What are his provisions for it?   2/ What is the change in man's diet? the stipulation?   3/ What makes Ham's actions so despicable?   4/ How does Noah react to Ham's actions (cursing the son of an offender reflects on the father)?   5/ How do you react to someone's sin against you?   6/ What do you think of someone who under the guise of "concern" spreads his conception of your weaknesses and sins? With God's help how can you be trusted to understand and take care of your fellow Christian's weaknesses?

### DAY 6   △   *Genesis 10*

1/ Why, do you think, does God give the names of so many "un-important" people? What do these name lists reveal about God?   2/ Project an historical record of you thousands of years hence. How would you like to be described?   3/ What phrase would accurately characterize your life thus far?   4/ In what area of your life today is the fact that God knows you by name and has a place for you important? 5/ How are the nations delineated here related to each other?

DAY 7 △ *Genesis 11:1-26*
1/ In what ways does pride and rebellion against God inevitably lead to an inability to understand and be understood by other men? 2/ In what areas of your life has this result of pride been evident? 3/ How and when do you "build" similar structures? Why? 3/ What are a-you and b-your Christian group "building" now?

DAY 8 △ *Genesis 11:27—12:19*
1/ What is God's attitude toward the Jews? What is yours? 2/ How have some of God's promises regarding the Jews already been fulfilled? 3/ How are you an active *blessing* to the people of Abram's promised seed? 4/ Trace Abram's travels on a map (continue in subsequent days). 5/ What prompts Abram's journey? his plan concerning Sarai? How does he fare because of the agreement? 6/ How does his lack of trust in God affect others? 7/ In what difficult areas is God calling you to trust him? How is your response affecting others?

DAY 9 △ *Genesis 13*
1/ What is Abram and Lot's problem? 2/ How does Abram resolve the problem? What does his handling of the problem reveal about his character? 3/ How does the way you settle differences and arguments reveal your trust (or lack of it) in God? 4/ What does Lot's choice reveal about his character? 5/ In view of God's clear will expressed to Abram what is your attitude toward Israel? How do you actually express your attitude?

DAY 10 △ *Genesis 14*
1/ What happens to the "innocent bystander" Lot? 2/ What are the dangers of close association with ungodly people? 3/ Imagine Lot's feelings after his rescue. 4/ Who is Melchizedek? How does he, a stranger to the group, have God's revelation? 5/ How do these two strangers, Abram and Melchizedek, respond to each other? 6/ In what ways do you limit the ways, times, and places God can get through to people? How do you act toward fellow Christians? 7/ Why does Abram refuse the war spoils?

DAY *11*  △  *Genesis 15*

1/ How does God encourage Abram?   2/ What is Abram's main concern?   3/ On what basis is Abraham declared righteous (i.e. right with God)?   4/ What land does God covenant to give the Jews? How large? What do they have today?   5/ What predictions and promises does God make while Abram is asleep (watch the future developments)?   6/ How do you show that you believe God's words to you?

DAY *12*  △  *Genesis 16*

1/ How do Sarai and Abram try to "push" God? What is their basic problem? Imagine the household situation.   2/ What are the usual results of becoming impatient with God's timing and trying to rush things?   3/ Why do you tend to ignore results when you act impatiently?   4/ Why, do you think, does God not strike them down for procuring, adultery, and child-snatching respectively?   5/ How does God treat Hagar (the Ishmaelites are the Arabs)? What do his actions reveal about his character and purpose?   6/ In what ways do your actions affect future generations?

DAY *13*  △  *Genesis 17*

1/ How does God identify himself here?   2/ Of what does the Abrahamic covenant consist?   3/ How are God's commands and promises related?   4/ How does Abraham respond to God's promises? to his commands? What do these responses reveal about Abraham?   5/ Imagine the feelings of Abraham and Sarah as they watch Ishmael grow up.   6/ What promises has God given you? How are you responding to them today?

DAY *14*  △  *Genesis 18*

1/ How does God appear to Abraham?   2/ How does Abraham treat the three men? Why?   3/ How does Sarah react to God's promise?   4/ What is God's reaction to the general sinfulness of Sodom and Gomorrah? Abraham's response to God's threat?   5/ From the dialogue of God and Abraham what do you learn about God? about intercessory prayer?

DAY *15*  △  *Genesis 19*

1/ Where is "innocent bystander" Lot?   2/ Characterize the men

28

of Sodom. What makes them so adamant concerning Lot and his godly friends? 3/ Explain Lot's predicament. 4/ Why don't Lot's relatives listen to him? Characterize his relatives as revealed by their actions. 5/ Describe the effect of this display of God's judgment on Lot. 6/ What are some of the immediate results of Lot's close association with the "swingers" of Sodom? Do you think his main motive has been to witness? 7/ Examine your influence on and witness to others. Do they understand your beliefs and respect your words? Why?

DAY *16*  △  *Genesis 20*

1/ What is Abraham's basic problem here (cf. 12:10-19)? 2/ In what areas of your life do you have repeated downfalls? Why? 3/ How does God show his faithfulness to a-Abraham and b-Abimelech? 4/ Why, do you think, are unchristian people sometimes more ethical than Christians? 5/ In what areas of your life are your ethics questionable? 6/ In what ways is Abimelech an example to follow?

DAY *17*  △  *Genesis 21*

1/ What "impossible" promise does God fulfill? 2/ What are some promises you have claimed? How can you be sure of them? 3/ Imagine Hagar's feelings as she is sent away. What provision does God make for her and Ishmael? 4/ How is Abraham including God more frequently in his relationships with others? What is happening to him? 5/ Why, do you think, does Abimelech believe that God is with Abraham—because of Abraham's conduct or God's faithfulness? 6/ What attribute of God is revealed by his name in verse 33?

DAY *18*  △  *Genesis 22*

1/ What makes this test extremely difficult? Imagine Isaac's feelings. 2/ What is God teaching Abraham about himself and his relationship to him? 3/ List some reasons God doesn't take Abraham's "sacrifice" after all. 4/ What does God really want from you? How does he typically treat your treasures when you are willing to offer them to him? 5/ What does this experience reveal about God's character? 6/ How does an experience as this reveal your concept of God?

DAY *19*  △  *Genesis 23*

1/ How must Abraham have behaved to arouse this response from strangers?   2/ What here should you imitate?   3/ Why, do you think, does Abraham insist on paying?   4/ Compare this incident and the one in 14:21-24. What qualities of Abraham do these incidents reveal?   5/ What is the difference between humility and "inferiority complex"? between humble independence and the inability to accept a gift?

DAY *20*  △  *Genesis 24*

1/ What makes Abraham so set against Isaac's intermarriage and even contact with the Canaanites?   2/ What does the servant believe about God in order to make the kind of prayer he makes?   3/ How does he show his faith by his subsequent actions? How does he know the will of God?   4/ How do Rebekah's relatives respond to the servant's request? Why doesn't Laban suspect the servant who wants to take his sister?   5/ How do you react to someone who tells you "God's will" concerning you?   6/ Characterize Rebekah and Isaac.

DAY *21*  △  *Genesis 25*

1/ Summarize what you have learned about Abraham, about his relationship with God, and about God's covenant with him.   2/ What does God predict about Rebekah's sons (watch the future developments)?   3/ Characterize Esau and Jacob. What about their characters and concerns does the incident in verses 29-34 reveal?   4/ What are the valued things and priorities in your life? Why?

DAY *22*  △  *Genesis 26*

1/ What does God promise Isaac? Why?   2/ What seems to be the attitude toward established personal relationships?   3/ What are some of Isaac's problems?   4/ How do you (or will you) influence your children to help them not repeat your sins?   5/ What kind of man is Abimelech turning out to be? What counterparts of his type are in today's world?   6/ Summarize what you have learned so far from *Genesis* about a-God, b-man, and c-yourself.

DAY *23*  △  *Luke 10:1-24*

1/ Summarize what Jesus has done for the people of the first nine chapters. 2/ How does Jesus intensify his ministry (cf. 9:1-6)? 3/ Do you pray in accordance with verse 2? 4/ Describe this realistic missionary preparation under these headings: the purpose, method, message and activity, conduct, result, and hearers' responsibility. 5/ How do these principles apply to your witness  6/ What is a-God's and b-man's part in man's understanding of God's truths?  7/ How are hearing and receiving Christians like hearing and receiving Christ?  8/ How is the opportunity for hearing related to the severity of judgment?  9/ How is God's omniscience necessary for his judgment?  10/ What facts reveal that Satan has lost his exalted power?  11/ What is the supreme cause for *rejoicing?* What makes Jesus rejoice?  12/ How are the persons of the trinity related?  13/ How are the disciples privileged? How are you?

DAY 24  △  *Luke 10:25-42*
1/ What are the law's requirements for eternal life? Have you done these? In what way do you have eternal life?  2/ How does this parable bring out the difference between knowledge and action?  3/ How does Jesus point out the segregation of the lawyer?  4/ Contrast the seeing, feeling, and activity of the three characters.  5/ Who is your *neighbor?* How can you be a *neighbor* to them today? What will be your basic attitude toward them?  6/ In what ways do you try to maintain a balance between quiet worship and practical service? How can you know which is more appropriate in a given situation?

DAY 25  △  *Luke 11:1-13*
1/ On what basis can a-the disciples and b-you approach God? Contrast this with the salutation and content of Jewish prayers (cf. 1:67-68).  2/ List and explain the specific concerns of the prayer.  3/ Are you asking the Lord to teach you to pray?  4/ What qualities of God are revealed by these parables?  5/ What are the two relationships pictured in verses 5-13?  6/ Compare the friend's answer (with possible mixed motives) with God's answer. 7/ Contrast the son's requests with the conjectures of supply. Compare the father's actual supply with God's supply.  8/ Imagine as a disciple how this prayer and the parables enlarge your concept of God.  9/ Is there any reason for hesitating to go to God in time of need? Is time a barrier to God's answering? How certain is his answer?

DAY *26*  △  *Luke 11:14-36*

1/ What are the responses to Jesus' miracle?  2/ How are *a*-Satan and *b*-God consistent in the way they work?  3/ What awkward double standard does Jesus reveal in the thinking of the Jews?  4/ Contrast the extent of *a*-Jesus' and *b*-the sons' power.  5/ What tremendous claims does Jesus make here?  6/ How does he show that neutrality in not an option?  7/ What is *a*-God's and *b*-your part in overcoming Satan and his devils?  8/ What is the outcome of mere renunciation of sins?  9/ Who, does Jesus say, is *blessed* (the woman's type of honoring expression is common—cf. 1:42)?  10/ What sign will be given to the people (the Ninevites regard Jonah as it were raised from the dead—cf. Jonah 1:11-17; 2:10)?  11/ How and why will *this generation* be judged (cf. 1 Kings 10: 1-14; Jonah 3)?  12/ How do verses 33-36 relate to the reason the Jews demand a sign?  13/ How does Jesus' use of the metaphor of *light* here differ from what he is illustrating in 8:16?  14/ What can you do to guard against the *light* in you becoming *darkness?*

DAY *27*  △  *Luke 11:37-54*

1/ How is the attitude of this Pharisee toward Jesus different from most Pharisees?  2/ Following through with the illustration of the cup and platter (the cleansing is ceremonial) describe the inside and outside of the Pharisees.  3/ What will and will not make the Pharisees *clean?*  4/ What is Jesus' attitude to outward forms and ceremonies?  5/ How does the Pharisees' hypocrisy affect other people (Jews mark graves to prevent unconscious defilement—cf. Num. 29:16)?  6/ In what ways does your inner life differ from your projected image? How can a discrepancy have a detrimental effect on others?  7/ What does Jesus condemn in the lawyers (cf. 2 Chron. 24:20-22—Chronicles is the last book of the Jewish canon)?  8/ What is the result of their sin concerning themselves? concerning other people?  9/What are modern counterparts of the Pharisees' and lawyers' sins?  10/ Imagine the kind of pressure Jesus endures during his lifetime.

DAY *28*  △  *Luke 12:1-12*

1/ In what ways is hypocrisy futile?  2/ What does Jesus tell his disciples that prepares them for the future?  3/ What *a*-encouragement and *b*-warning does he give them?  4/ Who will *a*-defend them, b-protect them, and c-guarantee their eternal destiny? 5/ Are *fear him* (v. 5) and *fear not* (v.7) contradictory? 6/ How do Jesus' words affect the content of your message to students, neighbors, associates, others? 7/ What is the awful result for people who refuse the witness of the Holy Spirit? 8/ How can this knowledge incite a-the disciples and b-you to a bold, persuasive witness?

DAY 29    △    *Luke 12:13-34*

1/ How does the man misunderstand Jesus' purpose? 2/ List what Jesus says about a-the attitudes apt to be produced by honest accumulation of earthly possessions (underline the pronouns in the parable), b-the right attitude toward possessions, c-God's estimate of the value of possessions (compare with the value of life), and d-what to do with possessions and why. 3/ How does a right view of possessions reflect a right view of God? 4/ How does Jesus reveal that God is concerned with the whole of man not just his soul? 5/ Why is *worrying* utterly worthless? 6/ In what ways are ravens, lilies, and grass (grass is used for fuel in Palestine) dependent on God? What principle do they illustrate? 7/ What does this passage teach about a-life and b-the kingdom of heaven? 8/ In what practical ways do you see God's concern for and value of you?

DAY 30    △    *Luke 12:35-59*

1/ How does the attitude toward the Lord's return reveal where a man's treasure (cf. v. 34) is? 2/ How can you be *ready* for the Lord's return? 3/ How are a-readiness and b-unreadiness manifest in the three parables in verses 35-48 (the typical long garments hinder activity)? 4/ What will be the result of a-readiness and b-unreadiness? 5/ How much more important is faithfulness than ability in measuring results? 6/ How are you using the abilities and opportunities God is giving you? 7/ In what ways does God's knowledge of your opportunities a-comfort and b-convict you? 8/ Characterize *fire*. What *baptism* is Jesus referring to? 9/ Contrast the peace the Jews expect to accompany the Messiah's coming with what Jesus brings. 10/ How are the people hypocrites in regard to interpreting signs? 11/ How are verses 58-59 an illustration of eternal destiny?

# MONTH 3

### DAY 1  △  *Luke 13:1-21*
1/ What is the basic question raised in verses 1-5? Who raises it? Why?  2/ Is this idea still prevalent today? What "superstitions" do you have about death?  3/ Contrast the reasons for *a*-present and *b*-final destruction.  4/ How do these verses relate to the parable of verses 6-9 (fig trees mature in three years)?  5/ What is the effect of freedom on the woman?  6/ In what ways are the Jews hypocrites regarding the law of the sabbath?  7/ List what the animals and the woman can claim as needs.  8/ What fact about the kingdom of God is Jesus illustrating with the metaphors of the *mustard seed* and *leaven?*  9/ What are the responsibilities of the *man* in verse 19 and the *woman* in verse 21?  10/ What are your responsibilities in relation to the kingdom of God?

### DAY 2  △  *Luke 13:22-35*
1/ Compare 9:51 and 10:1 with verse 22.  2/ How does Jesus answer the academic question, How many will be saved?  3/ What is his main concern (*strive* refers to strenuous wholehearted determination)?  4/ What do the *workers of iniquity* misunderstand about entering the door? What are the consequences?  5/ How will the situation of verses 28-30 be amazingly dreadful for the Jews?  6/ On what do many today base the careless assumption that they are Christians?  7/ On what basis will you be admitted?  8/ Is Jesus absorbed with preoccupations and self pity as his death approaches (*the third day* is a poetic expression meaning at the time of completion)?  9/ Imagine how you would feel.  10/ What qualities of Jesus are revealed by his attitude here?  11/ In what ways are you conscious of your purpose in life? How do you express that purpose?

### DAY 3  △  *Luke 14:1-24*
1/ What, do you think, motivates Jesus to accept this social invitation?  2/ Do you give prayerful planning and concern to your social and recreational life? How can you meet the need of others during these times?  3/ Who determines the placing of the guests?  4/ Contrast man's self concept with the judgment of God.  5/ What is the right attitude of hospitality?  6/ What are your motives in planning a dinner or party? What kind of people do you invite (the tense of *invite* in v. 12 refers to *continually*)? What

about foreign students, the disliked, unattractive, and poorly dressed? 7/ What does one of the Pharisee's guests falsely assume (cf. v. 14)? 8/ In what ways is the invitation inclusive (cf. who finally comes)? 9/ In what ways are the excuses ridiculous? On what basis are the people excluded? 10/ What is the principle of this parable?

DAY 4  △  *Luke 14:25-35*

1/ What is significant in the Lord's addressing these words to the great multitude desirous of following him (cf. 9:57-62)? 2/ List and explain the demands of following Jesus (cf. each with v. 33). 3/ In what ways may your attitude toward Jesus *cost* yourself (the man bearing the cross expects to be crucified)? others (determine the meaning of *hate* in v. 26)? 4/ Compare or contrast the content of your attitude and message with Jesus' message here. 5/ How is the man who ignores the totality of Jesus' demands like saltless salt?

DAY 5  △  *Luke 15:1-32*

1/ Contrast the attitude of *a*-the Pharisees and *b*-Jesus toward sinners. 2/ To whom does Jesus address these stories? Under what circumstances? 3/ What is the unifying theme of the three? 4/ What are their distinctive features? What do each emphasize about the search? 5/ What is the attitude at the completion of the search (vv. 5-7, 9, 23-24, 32)? 6/ How, do you think, do Jesus' announcements of what happens in heaven affect his listeners? What do these announcements reveal about Jesus? 7/ Contrast the attitude of the son before he leaves and after he returns. What causes him to return? What is the essential change in him? 8/ How can rebellion sometimes lead to worse subordination? 9/ What is the elder brother's self concept? Do you think he is necessarily good or just afraid to outwardly rebel? 10/ Compare the father's attitude toward both sons. 11/ What is *a*-God's and *b*-man's part in spiritual restoration? 12/ In what ways have you experienced the qualities of God revealed by Jesus in these stories?

DAY 6  △  *Luke 16:1-13*

1/ Who is addressed here? Who overhears (cf. v. 14)? 2/ Describe the steward's business practices and motives. In what ways does he protect himself against a legal suit if found out?  3/ Explain what the rich man commends in his steward.  4/ In what ways does a misunderstanding of the principles of 12:22-34 parallel the charges in verses 1 and 8?  5/ What is your attitude toward your possessions?  6/ In what ways do you use them to *make friends?* to repulse people?  7/ How do these verses reveal the fallacy of the concept: you can be ethical in major responsibilities but fudge in small details?  8/ What is the relation of character and principles in everyday affairs with character and principles in "spiritual" affairs?  9/ How is your use of your possessions related to eternity?  10/ Contrast the attitudes, motives, and actions of people who *serve a*-God and *b*-mammon.  11/ Which *master* do you *serve?* How is your service reflected in your daily living?

DAY 7  △  *Luke 16:14-31*

1/ Contrast the attitude of *a*-Jesus (cf. vv. 9-13) and *b*-the Pharisees (they regard riches as a reward for their law abiding).  2/ Explain what Jesus means by *violently* here. How have you entered the kingdom of God?  3/ Does the gospel void the law (cf. 10:25-28)? Contrast Jesus' statement in verse 18 with Jewish morality of the time.  4/ Compare the parable of the rich man and Lazarus with Jesus' statement in verse 15.  5/ Contrast the life and death of each. How are their positions reversed?  6/ How does this parable show the seriousness of your attitudes and actions during your life?  7/ What is the principle of the parable?

DAY 8  △  *Luke 17:1-19*

1/ What two truths does Jesus emphasize concerning sin and responsibility for sin?  2/ What is your attitude toward sin and sinning brothers? Do you practice the aspect of forgiveness taught in verses 1-4?  3/ What are you doing about the quality of your faith (cf. the characteristics of a mustard seed in 13:18-19)?  4/ What is the effect of this kind of faith (sycamine trees have powerfully gripping roots)?  5/ As a servant what is the right attitude to service and its rewards?  6/ What do you expect from and give to God?  7/ What two commendable qualities are found in all ten lepers?  8/ Why, do you think. doesn't Jesus give the leprosy back to the nine?  9/ How are thanks and *praise to God* related?  10/ How will you show your gratitude to God today?

DAY 9  △  *Luke 17:20-37*

1/ Imagine the Jewish interest in the Messiah's kingdom (relate this to their political situation).  2/ In what ways does the kingdom differ from their expectations?  3/ How does a realistic understanding of the kingdom of God prevent gullibility in regard to predictions?  4/ Describe the situation before and after the final revelation of the Son of man.  5/ What principle do Noah (cf. Gen. 6:11-22) and Lot (cf. Gen. 19:12-26) exemplify?  6/ How will the final revelation disregard human intimacy and ties?  7/ Relate the proverb in verse 37 with the inquiry about *where* the people will be left.  8/ Measure the purposes and consequence of your life with verse 33.

DAY 10  △  *Luke 18:1-8*

1/ How should *a*-the disciples and *b*-you act when the coming of the Lord seems delayed?  2/ What is the one lesson the story about this judge teaches about God?  3/ Contrast the motives of *a*-the judge and *b*-God in answering prayer. What are their different attitudes toward people who come to them?  4/ Describe the woman's actions. Do you think it is easy for her to keep coming to the judge? Why?  5/ From verses 7-8 what do you learn about God's timing?  6/ Describe the situation of the earth when the Son of man finally comes (cf. 17:26-30).  7/ In view of the earth's situation relate God's *delay* and *speed*.  8/ How do you reveal your perseverance? Can you maintain faith over the long haul?

DAY 11  △  *Luke 18:9-17*

1/ How is the Pharisee's view of himself and others related? different?  2/ What are the negative and positive (the law requires tithing of only certain kinds of income) aspects of his actions?  3/ Why, do you think, does God despise a haughty self concept so much (cf. v. 14 with 14:11; 16:15)?  4/ What are the attitude and actions of the tax collector?  5/ How can you *humble yourself* rightly?  6/ What do your public and private prayers reveal about your character? about your concept of others?  7/ Why, do you think, do intelligent adults have a hard time *trusting* as children? In what other ways can you *receive the kingdom of God* as a child?

DAY 12  △  *Luke 18:18-30*

1/ What point is Jesus making clear by questioning the ruler's use of *good* in his address?    2/ What does the ruler misunderstand about the true fulfillment of the law?    3/ If this man is willing to do so much for his eternal life, why, do you think, doesn't he *sell all?* 4/ Why, do you think, is it *hard* for the rich to enter the kingdom of God? How is it possible?    5/ Imagine the feelings which prompt the question in verse 26 (cf. the Jewish concept that riches = God's favor; poverty = God's punishment).    5/ Does giving up possessions guarantee eternal life?    6/ What are your motives in following Christ?

DAY *13*  △  *Luke 18:31-43*
1/ What additional facts does Jesus now give the disciples about his future (cf. 9:22, 44)? Imagine why these words are so incredible to them.    2/ Imagine the life situation of the blind man.    3/ Why, do you think, do the people tell him to be quiet?    4/ In what ways can you be guilty of similar *rebuking?*    5/ Why, do you think, does Jesus ask such an obvious question?    6/ What qualities of Jesus are revealed by his actions in regard to the blind man?    7/ For what kind of happenings do you *give praise to God?*

DAY *14*  △  *Luke 19:1-10*
1/ What is Zacchaeus' attitude toward Jesus? List specific phrases. 2/ What is the people's attitude toward the event (cf. 5:27-32; 7:39-42; 15:1-2)?    3/ What, do you think, about Jesus' life prompts Zacchaeus' great change?    4/ Imagine the effect of these actions on the people concerned.    5/ In what ways does your *salvation* have practical and restorative outreach?    6/ Do you expect sinners to be saved or do you really expect only religiously inclined people to be interested?

DAY *15*  △  *Luke 19:11-28*
1/ Describe the situation which prompts this parable.    2/ Recall to whom Jesus is telling this parable.    3/ What will the lord's return mean to his servants?    4/ Relate the rewards to the nobleman's command.    5/ On what basis is a servant called *good* and another *wicked?*    6/ What kind of concept does the *wicked* servant have of the lord?    7/ What will the lord's return mean for his enemies (vv. 14, 27)?    8/ How does the Lord make clear in this parable that he will not set up his kingdom immediately?    9/ What do you learn here about the authority of the Lord?    10/ What do

you anticipate at the Lord's return in light of verse 26?    11/ What
is your concept of God as reflected in your obedience and service?

DAY *16*  △  *Luke 10:1–19:28*
1/ Summarize the ways in which Jesus is influencing a-his disciples,
b-the multitudes and individuals, and c-the Jewish religious leaders.
2/ How is the split between Jesus and the Jewish leaders becoming
more and more apparent?    3/ Group the parables according to a-
whom addressed and b-topics.    4/ Summarize what you have
learned about a-the kingdom of God, b-Jesus' purpose on earth, and
c-the demands of following (serving) Jesus.

DAY *17*  △  *Genesis 27:1-45*
1/ Briefly summarize Isaac's life before this event.    2/ What kind
of person is Jacob? Esau? Rebekah?    3/ How do the people regard
oral blessings and promises? How binding is Isaac's original blessing?
What problem results?    4/ How do you feel about breaking your
word (especially when you have been tricked)?    5/ Contrast the
content of the two blessings.

DAY *18*  △  *Genesis 27:46–28:22*
1/ How does Esau try to regain his lost favor with Isaac?    2/ What
does God promise Jacob? How has some of it been fulfilled?    3/
What is Jacob's response to God's presence? Why?    4/ What is
Jacob's concept of God as revealed by his vow at Bethel?    5/ When
and why do you make similar "agreements" with God?

DAY *19*  △  *Genesis 29*
1/ Trace Jacob's travels on a map (continue in subsequent days.)
2/ In what ways is Laban a hypocrite?    3/ Where do you see
God's concern for the underdogs in this passage?    4/ In what ways
is God teaching Jacob?    5/ What counterparts does Jacob have
today?

DAY *20*  △  *Genesis 30*
1/ In what ways do a-Jacob, b-Rachel, c-Leah, and d-Laban show
an understanding of God's omnipotence and sovereignty?    2/ Describe the homelife and parental influences Jacob's twelve sons are
coming under.    3/ Compare and contrast Jacob's pledge of honesty
(v. 33) with his actions. What is the difference between shrewdness

and cheating?   4/ How are you relating now to someone who has wronged you?

### DAY 21   △   Genesis 31

1/ How does Jacob know he should return to Canaan?   2/ Compare and contrast Jacob's report of the situation with the feelings of Laban and his sons.   3/ What is Rachel and Leah's opinion of their father?   4/ What is strange about Laban's talk of God and his gods (rights to the family inheritance)? How does this account for some of his behavior?   5/ What is the significance of the covenant at Mizpah (contrast with its popular use)?   6/ In God's dealings with Jacob, what do you learn about God's character? about his dealings with sinners? with you?

### DAY 22   △   Genesis 32

1/ In what ways has God shown love and faithfulness to Jacob? 2/ In what way is Jacob trying to take care of the situation with Esau? What do these actions reveal about Jacob's character?   3/ What occurs during Jacob's struggle with the man? What does this incident reveal about God?   4/ What is Jacob learning about a-himself and b-God?

### DAY 23   △   Genesis 33

1/ Contrast this meeting of the brothers with their previous life together.   2/ What has happened to Esau in the meantime? to Jacob? 3/ What can you learn here about resolving conflicts with others? What positive action can you do today to help resolve a conflict with someone?   4/ How does Jacob deceive Esau again?   5/ What is significant about the name of the altar (cf. 32:9)?

### DAY 24   △   Genesis 34

1/ What is the temptation presented to Jacob? How does he meet it?   2/ Why do Jacob's sons react so strongly?   3/ Contrast the main concerns of a-Hamor, b-Shechem, c-Jacob's sons, and d-Jacob. 4/ Characterize each as revealed by their actions.   5/ How does God's attitude toward intermarriage of his followers and those who don't know him affect your dating and courtship patterns?

### DAY 25   △   Genesis 35

1/ Basically what has happened to Jacob between his first encounter with God at Bethel and his return? 2/ What has gone wrong? Why? What has he finally learned? 3/ What else happens to affect Jacob during this crisis period? 4/ How are God's promises being fulfilled in and through Jacob? What do you learn here about God's character? 5/ What has happened since your first real encounter with God?

### DAY 26  △  Genesis 36

1/ What marks the differences between the families, possessions, and attitudes of Esau and Jacob? In what lands do they settle? 2/ What have you learned about the differences in their characters? List specific qualities of each. 3/ In what ways are these qualities passed on to their children? 4/ What difference does realizing that your "small" evil actions today can have long-term, far-reaching implications make in your living?

### DAY 27  △  Genesis 37

1/ How is Joseph tactless in his relations with people? How do most people, not only brothers, react to such a person? What kind of person is Joseph now? 2/ What are the problems of Jacob's other sons? Who are responsible? 3/ To what extent are you responsible for the effect in your life of other people's sins against you? 4/ In what ways is Jacob at fault in the whole situation? What are the consequences for him? for Joseph?

### DAY 28  △  Genesis 38

1/ What is Onan's sin (this custom is levirate marriage)? 2/ What kind of man is Judah? What "double standard" is evident here? 3/ What kind of person is usually severest in his treatment of a sinner? What about your character do your attitudes to the sins of others reveal? 4/ How is Tamar more righteous than Judah (when there are no brothers-in-law to perform the levirate duty, the father-in-law has the responsibility)?

### DAY 29  △  Genesis 39

1/ What kind of man is Joseph becoming? In what areas of his life is God *with him?* 2/ Describe his apparent work habits. What opinion do your employers and teachers have of you? Why? 3/ How does Joseph overcome temptation? 4/ Does faithfully following God guarantee a trouble-free life? 5/ What do you do when

41

you are wrongly accused? What is your attitude toward people who believe the accusation?

### DAY 30  △  *Genesis 40*
1/ How does Joseph make use of his circumstances? Imagine yourself in the situation. What is your probable reaction?   2/ How does Joseph behave toward those who don't know God?   3/ What is Joseph's concept of God? How is he an example for you today?

## MONTH 4

### DAY 1  △  *Genesis 41*
1/ What is the place of dreams in guidance? Why, do you think, does God give Pharoah advance warning in such a way?   2/ How does this event help Joseph?   3/ In what ways is Joseph concerned for the welfare of his enemies the Egyptians? How does Joseph's concern and ability to convey God's thought affect Pharaoh?   4/ In what ways does your witness to those around you affect the world?

### DAY 2  △  *Genesis 42*
1/ What circumstances bring about the meeting of Joseph and his brothers?   2/ What has happened to Joseph's brothers in the meantime? How do they feel about their past crime and God's activity? 3/ How is Joseph testing his brothers?   4/ What kind of person is Reuben (cf. 35:22; 37:21-30)?   5/ What do you learn here about God and his work through men to help you in your prayer life? in today's circumstances?

### DAY 3  △  *Genesis 43*
1/ How is God dealing with Jacob? How is he responsible for his sons' behavior and its present consequences?   2/ What is his attitude toward the loss of his children? What is yours?   3/ What kind of influence is Joseph having politically and personally in Egypt? in the surrounding lands?   4/ What shows that Joseph is not compromising his convictions about God in Egypt (cf. previous chaps.)? 5/ To what extent does he adopt the mores of Egypt? To what extent should you practice the mores of your culture?

### DAY 4  △  *Genesis 44*
1/ In what way are Joseph's dreams (chap. 37) fulfilled here?   2/

What is God teaching a-the brothers and b-Jacob through Joseph?
3/ Characterize Judah (cf. 37:26-27; chap. 38; 43:3-10). 4/
What is your attitude toward those questionable deeds of yours done
in the past that no one knows about? Do you wait in fear for God's
retribution or do you confess them?   5/ What should be a Christian's attitude toward sorrow? What is yours?

### DAY 5   △   Genesis 45

1/ For what is God responsible? How far, practically, does God's
sovereignty extend? How are the brothers responsible?   2/ What is
your attitude right now to your particular circumstances? What is
Joseph's?   3/ Imagine the brothers' conversation on the way home.
What is Jacob's response to the news?

### DAY 6   △   Genesis 46

1/ How does Jacob know, despite the promise regarding Canaan,
that he should settle his family in Egypt?   2/ Imagine the reunion
of father and son. In what ways has each changed over the years?
3/ How is Joseph, familiar with the Egyptian scene, trying to insure
Israel's separation?   4/ Distinguish separation from isolation.

### DAY 7   △   Genesis 47

1/ How does Jacob sum up his life?   2/ Describe the extent of the
famine.   3/ How does Joseph show compassion to an alien people?
With what economic principles does he deal with the hungry and
underprivileged? What is their response to him?   4/ What qualities do you reveal in your vocation and everyday duties?

### DAY 8   △   Genesis 48

1/ What do you learn about God here?   2/ How does Jacob sum
up his life here (contrast his summation in chap. 47)?   3/ In what
ways are the predictions for Ephraim and Manasseh similar to the
predictions and fulfillment for Jacob and Esau? (cf. 25:21-34; chap.
27)?   4/ What is Jacob's perspective in this situation?   5/ How
do you look at present circumstances—politically, socially, and personally—in the light of God's announced plans? To what extent do
you look for God's further deliverance?

### DAY 9   △   Genesis 49

1/ On what basis does Jacob predict his sons' futures (follow their

43

careers in later Jewish history)? Compare his summation of their characters with what you have learned about them. List and explain the metaphors he uses to describe them.  2/ In what ways is Judah singled out?  3/ What kind of future, especially spiritual, would someone who knows you well predict for you?

DAY *10*  △  *Genesis 50*

1/ What are Joseph's relations with Pharaoh?  2/ How does Joseph feel about defending himself or taking revenge?  3/ Summarize Joseph's influence on *a*-the people of Egypt and the surrounding lands and *b*-his family.  4/ In what ways are you influencing those around you?  5/ Summarize how the Israelites come to be in Egypt. What are Jacob's and Joseph's predictions for Israel (cf. vv. 24-25 with 48:21—follow the fulfillment in *Exodus*)?

DAY *11*  △  *Luke 19:29-48*

1/ Summarize the main thrusts of Jesus' teaching from the first nineteen chapters.  2/ Describe the entry into Jerusalem. What part do each of the following have: Jesus, the disciples, the multitudes? Imagine their feelings (recall their views of the kingdom of God). 3/ What is the significance of getting the colt (cf. Zech. 9:9)?  4/ Why, do you think, do the Pharisees want Jesus to rebuke his disciples (relate to their political situation)?  5/ What does Jesus' answer reveal as to his consciousness of his identity?  6/ What do the multitudes misunderstand about *peace* (cf. vv. 38, 42-44 with the destruction of Jerusalem in A.D. 70)?  7/ What is Jesus' attitude when he speaks judgment?  8/ In what ways does Jesus show authority?  9/ What is your purpose in the world in relation to history? In what ways does this knowledge of your purpose give you courage in the face of opposition?

DAY *12*  △  *Luke 20:1-18*

1/ Imagine the Pharisees' reaction to Jesus' reform in the temple (cf. 19:45-46).  2/ In what ways is there a conflict of authority between the religious leaders and Jesus?  3/ How does the Pharisees' plan to reveal this conflict backfire?  4/ Think through their motives for asking their question and not answering Jesus' question. What do these motives reveal about their character?  5/ How does Jesus reveal that he knows their motives?  6/ Relate the parable to the past and future history of the Jewish nation (cf. Isa. 5:1-7;

Luke 11:46-52; 13:32-35; 9:22; 19:42-44).  7/ In what areas of your life do you recognize Jesus' authority?

### DAY *13*  △  *Luke 20:19-26*
1/ Describe the leaders with at least three adjectives.  2/ What new methods do they employ to trap Jesus?  3/ In what ways will the spies' question not arouse the people's suspicion?  4/ Contrast the content of the spies' words with their motives for what they say. 5/ In what ways is Jesus' answer appropriate in view of *a*-the political and religious situation and *b*-his teaching?  6/ In what ways do state and church concerns seem to conflict today? What is your moral obligation in each case?

### DAY *14*  △  *Luke 20:27-47*
1/ What is the basis for the Sadducees' question (cf. Deut. 25:5-10)?  2/ In what two ways have they completely misunderstood the resurrection (v. 35)?  3/ How does Jesus show that Moses (the Sadducees believe that Moses never teaches the resurrection) refers to the truth of the resurrection (cf. Ex. 3:6)?  4/ What is the basic error of the Jewish leaders regarding Jesus' identity (cf. 3:31)?  5/ On what do you base your answers to religious and practical issues? 6/ Characterize the scribes.  7/ List modern counterparts of their characteristics.  8/ In what ways do you make a *pretense* of piety?

### DAY *15*  △  *Luke 21:1-19*
1/ In what ways does the widow give *more*?  2/ In what ways may you be tempted to cite injustices done to you (cf. 20:47) as an excuse for sacrificing (cf. 21:2-4)?  3/ Imagine the splendor of the temple and the effect of Jesus' words.  4/ What are the *a*-political, *b*-natural, *c*-religious, and *d*-personal *signs*? Relate verse 13 to these events.  5/ How does Jesus' refutation of his opponents strengthen the promise of verse 15?  6/ How does this discourse enlarge on 12:4-12?  7/ What quality must the disciples possess? 8/ How are you revealing this quality in your daily living?

### DAY *16*  △  *Luke 21:20-38*
1/ What is the reason for the destruction of Jerusalem (cf. 11:50; 19:43-44)? Describe and imagine the desolation.  2/ In what way does Jesus enlarge the scope of his predictions?  3/ Contrast the purpose of what will happen to *a*-Jerusalem (v. 22) and *b*-the world

(v. 28).   4/ What attitudes and events can be clearly known and expected (cf. the parable from nature)?   5/ What specific commands are given to govern life in the meantime (cf. v. 36 with v. 19)?   6/ How certain are these predictions (cf. v. 8)?   7/ Contrast Jesus' birth and his return as to the effect on people (cf. v. 27 with 1:31-33; chap. 2). Compare the business as usual preceeding both events (esp. 12:40; 17:26-30).   8/ How seriously do you take these predictions?   9/ How does your faith in the Son of man overcome *fear* and *foreboding?*   10/ Distinguish a realistic expectation of future events from pessimism.

### DAY *17* △ *Luke 22:1-20*

1/ What is *a*-Satan's and *b*-Judas' part in the betrayal of Jesus?   2/ Relate verses 5-6 and verse 2.   3/ In what ways are you aware of Satan's power in individuals today (cf. 17:1-3)?   4/ Imagine the suspense and intrigue of this last week in view of Jesus' knowledge of Judas' plan and his final teaching (cf. 21:37-38; v. 15).   5/ What precautions does Jesus make about the place for the passover (only women carry water jars)?   6/ Imagine what you say to your family and friends if it is your last meal together (but they don't realize it).   7/ What is the significance of the Lord's passover supper (cf. v. 7; Ex. 12:1-20)?

### DAY *18* △ *Luke 22:21-38*

1/ Contrast the concerns of *a*-the disciples (v. 24) and *b*-Jesus (vv. 14-19).   2/ In what way is leadership among Christians different from the current concept of authority? Describe the qualities and attitudes of a Christian leader.   3/ In what ways does Jesus show his knowledge of *a*-Satan, *b*-Simon, *c*-the future, and *d*-meeting Satan's attacks?   4/ How can you strengthen others to meet temptation?   5/ What reception have the disciples gotten previously because of their connection with Jesus as an honored teacher (cf. chaps. 9-10)? In what ways will this reception change?   6/ What do the disciples misunderstand about Jesus' meaning of *sword?*   7/ What is your defense in the face of opposition?

### DAY *19* △ *Luke 22:39-53*

1/ Describe the pressures on *a*-Jesus and *b*-his disciples. How does each deal with them?   2/ What is Jesus' main concern for *a*-himself and *b*-his disciples?   3/ What is the chief obstacle to the dis-

ciples' praying?    4/ What pressures do you have? How do you deal
with them? Why?    5/ Imagine the two companies meeting. What
shows that Jesus submits voluntarily to the powers of darkness?

### DAY 20   △   *Luke 22:54-71*

1/ Imagine the disciples' feelings after the event on the Mount of
Olives.   2/ Imagine the gossip in the courtyard about the new
prisoner. How does Peter handle the awkward situation he is in?
3/ How do you act when you realize you have denied Christ in a
difficult situation? Why?    4/ How is Jesus treated psychologically
and physically (cf. 18:32)?    5/ What is the council trying to get
Jesus to "admit"? When they succeed, how do they act?    6/ Why,
do you think, does Jesus give a clear affirmative answer here (cf.
4:18-22;  5:20-26;  6:5;  9:18-22;  20:9-18,  41-44)?

### DAY 21   △   *Luke 23:1-12*

1/ Although the Jewish council want to put Jesus to death because
he claims to be the Son of God (the charge—blasphemy), what
charges do they bring before Pilate?    2/ Imagine the Roman-Jewish
relations. What about the charges can make Pilate suspicious of their
validity?   3/ What about the accusations is false?    4/ Account for
the "politics" of Pilate after his statement of verse 4.   5/ What is
Herod's attitude toward Jesus (cf. 9:7-9)?    6/ In what ways do
you try to avoid making decisions? Why? Does it work?

### DAY 22   △   *Luke 23:13-31*

1/ What about Jesus is repeatedly stressed in this passage?    2/
What makes Pilate back down on his original verdict (cf. v. 4—
chastising is a preliminary to a prisoner's crucifixion)?    3/ Imagine
the mob hysteria.   4/ What kind of man is Barabbas?    5/ In what
ways are your decisions a result of your convictions? of popular
opinion and demand?    6/ Imagine Jesus' physical condition from
the agony on the Mount of Olives, the all-night trial, and the chastise-
ment.   7/ What perspective does Jesus try to give the mourning
women? Imagine the effect of Jesus' words (cf. the Jewish feeling
toward barrenness—1:7, 24-25).

### DAY 23   △   *Luke 23:32-43*

1/ Visualize the scene and the characters. What are the attitudes of
the people and soldiers toward Jesus?    2/ What does Jesus pray?

For what purpose?   3/ What is the significance of the inscription?
4/ Contrast the attitudes revealed by the requests of the two criminals. What kinds of deliverance are they seeking?   5/ What, do you
think, about Jesus makes such an impression on one criminal?   6/
What kind of people do you usually regard as impenetrable to the
gospel?   7/ Contrast the people's attitude toward the criminals with
Jesus' attitude toward them.

DAY *24*   △   *Luke 23:44-56*

1/ Describe the natural and religious phenomena that accompany
Jesus' death.   2/ What are the various reactions of the people to
these events? What is common among them?   3/ What is the significance of Jesus' death for you? What is your response?   4/ Characterize Joseph. What do he and the women do after Jesus' death?
5/ Contrast the actions of Joseph and the women with the attitudes
and actions of the people in the first part of chapter 23. What makes
the difference?

DAY *25*   △   *Luke 24:1-12*

1/ Who are the first to discover the fact that Jesus is raised from
the dead?   2/ Are you discovering daily the life of Christ because
you seek him through acts of love?   3/ Imagine the women's con-
fusion at the angels' question in verse 5.   4/ To what "proof" of
Jesus' resurrection do the angels refer (cf. vv. 6-7 with 9:22, 18:31-
33)?   5/ What is the natural response to such a discovery?   6/
Imagine yourself one of the women. What do you say to try to convince the despondent disciples of Jesus' resurrection?   7/ How do
the disciples respond to the news (cf. 9:45, 18:34)?   8/ Who will
you tell that Christ is alive today?

DAY *26*   △   *Luke 24:13-35*

1/ Imagine the disciples' reaction at the intrusion of a "stranger"
while they discuss such things.   2/ What about their attitude
toward Jesus is revealed by what they tell the "stranger"?   3/ How
does Jesus explain the events?   4/ What motive for Bible study
does this give you? Do you know what is written about him by the
prophets?   5/ List the factors which contribute to the disciples'
recognition of Jesus.   6/ What is their response to their new knowledge?   7/ What is your basic way of gaining knowledge of Christ?

8/ What marks the turn of events in this passage? Contrast the countenance and attitudes of the disciples before and after.

### DAY 27   △   Luke 24:36-53
1/ What is the psychological state of the disciples when Jesus appears to them?   2/ With what kinds of evidence of his resurrection is Jesus concerned?   3/ What is the disciples' part in the evidence? How will they be able to fulfill their part?   4/ Trace the progression in the disciples' understanding and response.   5/ What is Christ's command to you today in your immediate situation? How will you be able to fulfill it?   6/ Are you asking God about his will for you in terms of *all nations?*   7/ Imagine you are a disciple. How does this event change your life?   8/ How does the fact of the resurrection affect your daily living?

### DAY 28   △   Luke 1—24
1/ In what ways does Luke keep his audience in mind throughout his book (cf. main Greek concerns)?   2/ In what ways does he portray Jesus' *a*-humanity and *b*-diety?   3/ Summarize the ministry and methods of Jesus.   4/ What is the purpose of Jesus' death and resurrection?   5/ In what ways does Luke convince you of *a*-the historic reality of Jesus' life and *b*-the truth of his teachings?

### DAY 29   △   *Introduction to the Psalms*
The *Psalms* are personal and public poems of worship used as hymns. They represent a range of emotional tones, subjects, and authors. Read the psalms aloud and imagine the experiences and feelings which prompt their writing. *Psalm 1*   1/ Contrast the righteous and the wicked.   2/ How are delight and meditation connected? Do you daily study and obey the word of God?   3/ What characteristics of the evergreen tree are given? How do these characteristics relate to the righteous man?   4/ How do you compare to the righteous man? What *fruit* is God producing in your life to nourish others? 5/ What presently in your life can be classified as *chaff?*   6/ Title this psalm as to content.

### DAY 30   △   *Psalm 2*
1/ Compare this and the first psalm.   2/ What are the actions and destiny of evil nations?   3/ How effective are the plots? What is

God's response to them?    4/ What is the author David's answer to the opposition against him as God's representative?    5/ How do you relate national and international crises to God? Is God sovereign? 6/ Contrast the activities of the nations with the purposes of God. 7/ What advice does the psalmist give the kings? Why?    8/ What is your relationship to the last statement in this psalm?    9/ Title this psalm as to content.

## MONTH 5

#### DAY 1  △  *Psalm 3*
1/ Compare 2 Samuel 15 (esp. vv. 12-13).    2/ Trace the concept of *deliverance* through this psalm.    3/ What is the significance of *but* in verse 3?    4/ To what extent are verses 5-6 true in your life? Why?    5/ Does the first half of verse 7 contradict verses 5-6? Give your reasons.    6/ List the problems confronting David in this psalm. List the solutions.    7/ How do these problems and solutions relate to your experience?    8/ Title this psalm as to content.

#### DAY 2  △  *Psalm 4*
1/ In the midst of this uprising to whom does David appeal?    2/ What charges does David make against the people?    3/ What exhortations does he give them?    4/ How does David speak of his relationship to God? How do you define your relationship to him? 5/ Explain the positive tone of verses 7-8. How does verse 8 relate to verse 5?    6/How can you *offer right sacrifices* today?    7/ Title this psalm as to content.

#### DAY 3  △  *Psalm 5*
1/ At what time of day is this prayer made?    2/ What evidence does this psalm give of the personal relationship between David and God?    3/ What is the significance of *watch* in verse 3?    4/ What answers do you expect from your prayers as you watch for them? 5/ On what basis is David's confidence as he makes request for his deliverance and his enemies' destruction (vv. 4-8)?    6/ Characterize evil-doers. Are any of these characteristics present in your life? 7/ What men have cause to anticipate the judgment of God? to rejoice?    8/ In the light of this psalm what is your present attitude? Why?    9/ Title this psalm as to content.

DAY *4*  △  *Psalm 6*

1/ Read this psalm aloud (Sheminith probably means an octave lower).   2/ What is its mood through verse 7? What happens in verses 8-10?   3/How do you know this is a *personal* psalm?   4/ What characteristics of distress do you find? of rejoicing?   5/Do you ever feel this way? Why?   6/ Compare verse 4 with verses 8-10. How can David speak with such assurance?   7/ How can you have assurance about your prayers?   8/Title this psalm as to content.

DAY *5*  △  *Psalm 7*

1/ How do verses 1-2 set the tone of this psalm?   2/ What is David doing in verses 3-5? What is he willing to have done to him if he is guilty?   3/ How does David picture God?   4/ What does he ask God to do?   5/ Characterize the wicked man (cf. vv. 1-2).   6/ How does verse 17 relate to the rest of the psalm?   7/ At what points can you identify with this psalm? Why?   8/ Title this psalm as to content.

DAY *6*  △  *Psalm 8*

1/ Compare verse 1 with verse 9. What purpose do these two verses have in the psalm?   2/ Can you include yourself in the use of *our*? Why?   3/ What things are said about God? about man? Compare and contrast God and man.   4/ What is the significance of the questions in verse 4? How does verse 4 relate to verse 3?   5/ How does verse 2 fit in with the remainder of this psalm?   6/ How would you describe and title this psalm? Why?

DAY *7*  △  *Psalm 9*

1/ In the opening verses what does David say he will do?   2/ Which of these are presently a part of your life?   3/ What is the experience of the enemies? Why?   4/ What is said about God?   5/ What reasons are given for praising God? Compare the use of *praise* in verses 2, 11, 14.   6/ Compare the *nations* and *wicked*.   7/ Contrast the enemy (vv. 15-17) and the Lord (vv. 7-12).   8/ Compare verse 18 with verses 15-17. What differences are given?   9/ In verses 19-20 whom is David calling God to judge?   10/ Considering the world situation to what extent can you make this your prayer?   11/ Title this psalm as to content.

DAY *8*   △   *Psalm 10*

1/ What problem is expressed here? Compare this and the ninth psalm.   2/ What is said about the attitude of the wicked? his actions? his relationship to God? How do his attitude and actions illustrate his belief of verses 4, 11?   3/ What does the psalmist ask God to do? On what basis does he appeal to God?   4/ List the characteristics of God's rule.   5/ Explain the last half of verse 18. What is significant about what it says?   6/ Contrast the present and final situations of man.   7/ Is verse 4 or 17 more appropriate to your life?   8/ Title this psalm as to content.

DAY *9*   △   *Psalm 11*

1/ In verse 1 what two sources of refuge are mentioned? Which does David choose?   2/ What is the target of the wicked? What do they hope to do (cf. 1 Sam. 18:10-11; 19:9-10)?   3/ Explain verse 3. How does this relate to what is said of the Lord in verses 4-7?   4/ What is the difference in God's dealing with the righteous and the wicked?   5/ How is God dealing with you now? Do you know why?   6/ Compare the three references to righteous and uprightness in verse 7. How is each related to God?   7/ Can a man see God? How have you seen him recently?   8/ Title this psalm as to content.

DAY *10*   △   *Psalm 12*

1/ What sin is expressed in verse 1?   2/ In verses 2-4 what is discussed? How many different sins are mentioned?   3/ Which of these weaknesses are present in your life? in society?   4/ Whom does God assist?   5/ What is the difficulty in verse 5? What does God say he will do?   6/ Contrast the words of God with the words of men.   7/ How does this difference encourage you to trust God?   8/ What is verse 8 saying? What evidences of this do you see today?   9/ Title this psalm as to content.

DAY *11*   △   *Introduction to Acts*

Luke continues his orderly account of the extension of Christianity through the apostles and the Holy Spirit. *Acts 1:1-12*   1/ How does Jesus spend his time on earth after he rises from the dead?   2/ What are his plans for the disciples? What concerns them (cf. their concern throughout *Luke*)? How does Jesus answer their questions?   3/ What do Jesus' disciples *see* and *hear* in verses 9-11?   4/ What does this passage reveal about God's plan for your life during the time between Christ's ascension and return? 5/ What divine resource has God provided for you? 6/ Are you aware of any specific way the Holy Spirit has empowered you recently to witness of Christ?

DAY *12*  △  *Acts 1:12-26*

1/ How do Jesus' disciples spend their time after Jesus leaves them? 2/ On what grounds does Peter declare that another apostle will be chosen? To what will the new apostle witness? 3/ How do scripture, prayer, and providence (the lots) have a part in the new selection? 4/ With which of these three things do the disciples begin when they want to discern God's will? 5/ On what basis will you make today's decisions?

DAY *13*  △  *Acts 2:1-13*

1/ In what ways is Jesus' promise (1:5, 8) fulfilled in this passage? 2/ Describe the physical manifestations of the Spirit's coming. 3/ How does the Holy Spirit empower these men to be witnesses to the whole world (locate the countries on a map) at this time? 4/ Describe the reactions of the crowd. 5/ What is the disciples' message? 6/ What message do you share as you witness to others? 7/ How can you find power to be an effective witness for Christ?

DAY *14*  △  *Acts 2:12-36*

1/ How does Peter answer the charge that the disciples are drunk? 2/ When people misunderstand your Christian life and witness, what should you do? 3/ Which aspects of God's plan concerning Jesus of Nazareth does God accomplish through men and which without men (vv. 22-24)? 4/ Paraphrase Peter's argument of verses 24-36 (cf. Ps. 16:8-11). What does he try to prove? 5/ In verses 32-36, what does Jesus do now that he has been made *both Lord and Christ?* 6/ What difference does the risen, ascended, active Christ make in your daily living?

DAY *15*  △  *Acts 2:37-47*

1/ How do people respond to Peter's address? Have you ever responded in this way? When? For what reason? 2/ What action does Peter urge? 3/ What evidence is in this passage that God is concerned to save entire families? Have you claimed the promises of

God for the other members of your family?   4/ List the aspects or
manifestations of the new life of those who receive Peter's word.
Which of these aspects characterize you?

### DAY 16  △  Acts 3:1-10

1/ How do Peter and John show their love to God and to men on
this day?   2/ Contrast what the lame man expects with what he
receives.   3/ How do the people involved in this miracle—Peter and
John, lame man, spectators—give glory to God?   4/ What has God
given you that you can share today with people in need?

### DAY 17  △  Acts 3:11-26

1/ What does Peter say about Jesus? Of what does Peter accuse the
crowd?   2/ Summarize how each verse of this passage is appropriate to the Jewish audience Peter is addressing.   3/ As you witness
of Christ, how can you make the message appropriate and meaningful to your audience?   4/ What does Peter say will be the result of
repentance?   5/ What kind of response does God expect to the
words of Jesus?   6/ In verse 25 what does Peter say about the
extent of God's gracious purposes? In what ways have you experienced these *blessings?*

### DAY 18  △  Acts 4:1-12

1/ Why do the priests and Sadducees arrest Peter and John?   2/
what question do the Jewish leaders ask them? How does Peter
answer it?   3/ List five things that Peter says about Jesus Christ.
Why does saying each to this audience require a Spirit-given boldness?   4/ When has God put you in a difficult situation and filled
you with his Spirit to testify of Christ? What has happened?

### DAY 19  △  Acts 4:13-31

1/ Why do the men of the council say nothing publicly in opposition
to Peter and John? Why are they concerned about them?   2/
Imagine yourself in the situation. How do you answer the warning
given? Compare your answer with the answer of Peter and John.
3/ List the different parts of the disciples' prayer. What is significant about its order?   4/ Describe the God in whom the disciples
believe as revealed by their prayer.   4/ In what way does faith
in such a God make their witness bold?   5/ How does God answer

their prayer?   6/ Do you usually pray for deliverance from trying circumstances or for boldness in them?

DAY 20   △   *Acts 1:1–4:31*

1/ Describe the early church's concerns, activities, and growth. 2/ What is its effect on people?   3/ Compare or contrast these characteristics of the early church with your church's fellowship and outreach. What needs changing? How?   4/ What place does the Old Testament have in the thought and action of the early church? 5/ Summarize the main thoughts in Peter's sermons.   6/ What place does the Bible have in your thought and actions?   7/ What causes the beginning of persecution? From whom?

DAY 21   △   *Acts 4:32-37*

1/ How do you feel about your possessions?   2/ In what ways is the filling of the Holy Spirit (v. 31) manifest in today's passage? 3/ Describe the apostles' testimony. Is this an accurate description of your testimony?   4/ Why are those who believe in no need?   5/ Describe the profound change in the disciples' mode of living.   6/ What is different about your life because you belong to the church?

DAY 22   △   *Acts 5:1-12*

1/ Precisely what is the lie that Ananias and Sapphira agree to tell the apostles?   2/ What do verses 3-4 teach about the identity of the Holy Spirit? Do you think of the Holy Spirit in this way?   3/ What is God's reaction to sin in the church? What happens to Ananias and Sapphira?   4/ What does this incident teach you about God?   5/ In what ways are you holding back from God?   6/ Have you been completely honest with other people during the last week? 7/ In what ways are you dishonest with God? Do you pray that he will help you to be honest?

DAY 23   △   *Acts 5:12-42*

1/ What happens after the church is filled with fear?   2/ Why do the Sadducees oppose what God is doing through the apostles? Have you ever opposed what God is doing through others for this reason?   3/ How are the disciples let out of prison? For what reason? When do they start to obey the angel's command?   4/ What is significant about the place where they teach?   5/ Contrast the fear of the temple officers with the boldness of Peter and the other apostles.    6/ What in Peter's bold words enrages the Jewish council?    7/ Why does Gamaliel advise caution about the treatment of the apostles? Are your plans and activities of God or of men?    8/ How do the apostles respond to their beating? How do you respond to trying times in your Christian life?

### DAY 24  △  Acts 6

1/ What growing pains does the early church experience?    2/ List the qualifications demanded of the seven who are chosen to serve tables. Would you require such qualifications for men with this duty? Why or why not?    3/ How does your Christian group select leaders?    4/ What is your attitude toward routine service?    5/ Describe the attitude of the twelve toward priorities in their lives.    6/ To what does God want you to give priority in your life?    7/ Can some responsibility you are now carrying in your Christian group be assigned to someone else?    8/ What are the practical results in Jerusalem after the church makes a division of labor?    9/ After the problem within the church is settled, what problem does the church now face from outside? Describe the methods employed by the church's enemies.    10/ What evidences God's presence with Stephen?    11/ Have you ever been in a situation similar to Stephen's? What have you done?

### DAY 25  △  Acts 7—8:1

1/ How does Stephen identify with the council?    2/ Is this an appropriate time for a history lesson? How well-acquainted are you with the way God has guided the people of Israel?    3/ List what Stephen says God has done.    4/ Summarize the interplay of God's speech and actions. Are the actions alone sufficient?    5/ How does history repeat itself in this chapter? In what situations are you resisting God's purposes for you?    6/ Contrast the council's reaction to Stephen's defense with Stephen's response to the council's rage. What makes the difference?

### DAY 26  △  Acts 8:2-25

1/ What causes the church to spread out to other regions? How do you regard such a happening to your Christian group?    2/ What do those who are scattered do?    3/ Contrast Philip (cf. 6:5) and Simon considering their reputation, results of their activity, and attitude toward the Holy Spirit.    4/ Why do you want the power of God in your life? 5/ How concerned are you about what the other Christians in your group think of you? What are your motives for being "spiritual"?

### DAY 27    △    Acts 8:26-40

1/ What instructions does Philip receive from the angel? 2/ How has God already prepared the eunuch to hear the message of Christ? In what ways has God prepared you for the gospel? 3/ How does Philip initiate the conversation? When does he start talking about the good news of Christ? 4/ What evidence does the eunuch give of believing the message? 5/ What is the last impression you have of him? Compare this with the last impression of Simon in yesterday's reading. 6/ Summarize what God does for the eunuch and for Philip. How does this encourage you to talk with someone today about Jesus?

### DAY 28    △    Acts 4:32—8:40

1/ What is the result of persecution for the church's outreach? 2/ List the various problems the church faces. How is each handled? 3/ What are the evidences of the Holy Spirit's work in the early church? 4/ Compare or contrast the results of the Holy Spirit's presence in the early church with the results of his presence in your church. 5/ Describe the people in these chapters (excluding those cited in sermons) as to a-personal characteristics, b-response to God, and c-service to others.

### DAY 29    △    Acts 9:1-31

1/ Visualize the change in Saul (cf. 7:58—8:3). 2/ List his before and after characteristics. 3/ Under what circumstances has Jesus confronted you? How have you responded? 4/ Why is Ananias hesitant about God's command? How does God answer him? How are you acting now about something God wants you to do for him? 5/ How do the events of verses 17-30 confirm and illustrate what God says to Ananias (vv. 15-16)? 6/ How has your commitment to Christ involved you in suffering? 7/ To what extent does your Christian group experience what the early church experiences in verse 31?

### DAY 30    △    Acts 9:32-43

1/ Who heals the paralyzed man? What is the result? 2/ What

are some of the good works and acts of love of Tabitha? What good works and acts of love will you do today?   3/ What evidences that Peter raises Tabitha to life by the power of God? What is the result? 4/ Has anyone ever believed in the Lord after seeing the power of God in your life?

## MONTH 6

### DAY 1  △  Acts 10:1-33a

1/ Characterize Cornelius. To what extent does he believe the revelation that God has given in the Old Testament?   2/ How, do you think, has Cornelius learned about the true God? Why does God send an angel to him (v. 4)?   3/ How does God prepare Peter for his encounter with this gentile army officer?   4/ Put yourself in Peter's place. Imagine some animal you hate to touch, much less eat. What are your thoughts, emotions, and reactions as a result of such a vision?   5/ How do the events in this chapter further Christ's purpose as expressed in 1:8?   6/ What feelings do you have toward a group on race that prevent you from entering whole-heartedly into Christ's purpose for the world?

### DAY 2  △  Acts 10:1-48

1/ What difference does the vision of the unclean animals make in Peter's personal contact with Cornelius?   2/ How does Peter's sermon (vv. 34-43) differ from his other sermons in this book (e.g. 2:14-36)?   3/ List the facts that Peter wants Cornelius to know about Jesus Christ.   4/ What must you do to receive forgiveness of sins?   5/ How does God show his pleasure with the preaching of Peter and the faith of Cornelius? What additional command does Peter give?

### DAY 3  △  Acts 11:1-18

1/ Who objects to Peter's contact with the Gentiles? What does Peter do when confronted with criticism? What do you do?   2/ How does the circumcision party respond to Peter's patient explanation of what has happened?   3/ What gift does God give the Gentiles as well as the Jews? Have you received this gift? How do you know?   4/ Who motivates men to repent? How does this affect your prayers? What is the outcome of repentance?   5/ How does your Christian group handle matters of contention? Can you discover from today's passage a way to handle contention which can result in glorifying God?

### DAY 4 △ Acts 11:19-30

1/ Categorize specifically what a-God and b-men do to spread the gospel. What is the result? To whom is the result attributed? 2/ Describe the relationship between the churches at Antioch and Jerusalem. How do they mutually aid one another? 3/ How is your Christian group related to other Christian groups? In what ways does your group show love and concern for Christians in other places? 4/ List what is said about Barnabas. What specific things does Barnabas do and say to help these new Christians? 5/ What principles of Christian giving can you discover from today's passage?

### DAY 5 △ Acts 12:1-19

1/ What does Herod do to James and Peter? How does the church respond? 2/ What instructions does the angel give Peter? When does Peter know that the events are not a dream? 3/ Imagine you are here. How do you respond to Rhoda's news and the sight of Peter? Is Rhoda's reaction different from that of the others? When has an answer to prayer surprised you? 4/ Compare your view of angels with what is said here. 5/ Contrast the outcome of Herod's persecution in the lives of a-James and b-Peter. Is death or deliverance equally acceptable to you?

### DAY 6 △ Acts 12:20-25

1/ What kind of man is Herod (cf. vv. 1-19)? What does God have to do to him? Why? 2/ How does this passage add to what you learned yesterday about angels? 3/ When you are in a position of leadership, how can you *give God the glory*? How important does God consider this? 4/ Describe the activity of God in the life of this unchristian ruler. Even though God permits him to do much that is harmful, what is the final outcome concerning the word of God? 5/ Does God still rule the lives of authorities? How does this affect your prayers? 6/ Summarize the growth of the early church geographically and ethnically in spite of religious opposition.

### DAY 7 △ *Introduction to Exodus*

God has made a covenant with Abraham (review Gen. 12:1-3, 7;

13:14-17; 15:13-16; 17:1-21), reiterated to Abraham's son and grandson (review Gen. 26:24; 28:13-15). According to God's prediction Abraham's descendants have become exiles in Egypt (skim Gen. 45-48). Moses now records their deliverance as a nation. *Exodus 1* 1/ How has the political climate changed since Joseph's death? What is the new Pharaoh's view of the situation? 2/ In what three ways does Pharaoh try to stem the population explosion? Account for his lack of success and need for more drastic measures. 3/ What is the Egyptian view of human life? 4/ Compare and contrast the attitude of *a*-the king, *b*-the Egyptians, and *c*-the Hebrew midwives toward the Israelites. 5/ How does the midwives' attitude toward God affect their attitude toward people? the king's edict? What is the effect of the midwives' obedience on themselves? the Israelites? Pharaoh? 6/ When in tension between fear of God and fear of people and human authority to whom do you give allegiance? When and in what ways has your obedience to God affected others?

DAY 8  △  *Exodus 2*

1/ How does one couple circumvent Pharaoh's edict? Imagine how you would have acted. Why? 2/ How do the two environments of home and palace contribute to Moses' education, training, and preparation for leadership? 3/ Recount your experiences which have contributed to your present work or future plans. What experiences do you sometimes regard as wasted? Evaluate your attitude toward these considering this passage. 4/ What circumstances lead to Moses' losing identity as a prince and becoming an exile? 5/ How has God used even your sins to accomplish his purpose for you? 6/ Describe the condition of the Israelite minority when the king dies. Where is God in this (underline and explain the verbs of vv. 24-25)? 7/ Have you felt as if life is too much? When? What have you done? What facts here can strengthen your confidence and faith in God and his plan when you face similar situations in the future?

DAY 9  △  *Exodus 3*

1/ Imaginatively contrast Moses as a prince with Moses as an exile. Describe the circumstances that bring him to the mountain of God. How does the Lord get his attention here? 3/ What does Moses learn of God's character and identity? What is significant about God's

name (cf. his previous titles: Gen. 17:1; 28:3; 35:11)?    4/ Relate
God's knowledge of the situation to his command to Moses.    5/ In
what ways is the Lord revealing to you the desperation of people?
What are you doing about it?    6/ List a—the two objections Moses
raises in this passage and b—God's answer to each. Test the reason-
ableness of each objection in the light of God's answers.    7/ Summarize the job God is giving Moses (as God previews it): his message to the elders and to Pharaoh; the responses. On what does the
success of the project rest?

### DAY 10    △    Exodus 4

1/ List two more objections Moses raises. What is God's reply to
each?    2/ What objections do you raise when God gives you a job?
How reasonable are they in view of his call and equipping?    3/
What is the purpose of the signs? What do these signs reveal about
God's attitude toward people who doubt his word or messengers?
4/ What is the basic objection with Moses (v. 13)?    5/ In what
recent situation have you given God reason to be angry with you?
Why?    6/ How does God counter Moses' refusal to be his spokes-
man?    7/ What is Moses' first step in obedience? Find the additional facts God gives him.    8/ How has God confirmed his call to
you after your initial obedience in a given situation?    9/ Account
for God's harsh dealing with Moses considering Genesis 17:9-14.
10/ What disobedience (by default or deliberate) in your life must
be dealt with before you can carry out God's orders?    11/ Which
objections that Moses has raised are voided in verses 27-31?

### DAY 11    △    Exodus 5—6:1

1/ In their first skirmish with Pharaoh what do Moses and Aaron
ask (the Israelites cannot sacrifice within Egyptian limits because
animals, esp. cows, are sacred to Egyptians—cf. 8:26)?    2/ What is
Pharaoh's attitude toward the God of the Hebrews (each god has
his own jurisdiction and circumscribed power)?    3/ What new demands does Pharaoh place on the people as a result?    4/ Reconstruct the dialogue between the foremen and Pharaoh. How have
the foremen viewed the new problem? What is Pharaoh's interpretation?    5/ What are the reactions of the people to increased forced
labor? of Moses to their criticism?    6/ How do you react to the
pressure of multiplied problems and criticism?    7/ Relate the suit-
ability of God's answer (6:1) to the problem.

DAY *12*   △   *Exodus 6:2-25*

1/ What new aspect of his being does God reveal through his name (cf. vv. 2-3 with 3:14-16)?  \2/ List the seven aspects of God's deliverance for Israel. Compare these with what he has done and will do for you.   3/ What difference does *a*—knowing that God is actively involved in history and *b*—knowing something of his overall plan make in your attitude toward life?   4/ Contrast the attitude of the Israelites now (v. 9) with their initial reaction to Moses and Aaron (4:31). Account for the difference.   5/ How are your convictions affected by circumstances?   6/ How is this request (vv. 10-13) to Pharaoh different from the previous one?   7/ In view of the hopeless situation in verse 12 why don't they quit?   8/ When confronted with a hopeless situation is your tendency to quit or to look for a solution?   9/ Determine the meaning of *uncircumcised* in this context.   10/ What is significant about the three life spans specifically recorded here (cf. Gen. 6:3)?

DAY *13*   △   *Exodus 6:26—7:24*

1/ How does God answer Moses' despairing plea? Who will really move Pharaoh?   2/ What effect will these actions ultimately have on the Egyptians?   3/ In what ways have non-Christians known God's identity through your actions?   4/ Contrast the power by which Aaron and the magicians perform their signs.   5/ What is the underlying reason for the plagues?   6/ Imagine how this first plague would affect your own senses and needs. Imagine how the plagues would affect the attitude of the Israelites.   7/ How is Pharaoh affected by the plague (the Nile god is a main object of worship)? by his people's needs?   8/ Relate Pharaoh's disobedience with *a*—his ignorance of God's identity (cf. v. 17 with 5:2) and *b*—his evaluation of himself.   9/ How is your obedience or disobedience contingent on your view of God? How can you have a more clear and accurate understanding of him?

DAY *14*   △   *Exodus 7:25—8:32*

1/ Begin an outline or chart of the plagues, noting their characteristics, physical effects, changes in intensity over previous ones, the realm over which God displays power, reaction of Pharaoh, etc.   2/ Though the magicians imitate Moses and Aaron, where does Pharaoh turn for relief?   2/ Why doesn't Moses seek immediate relief since Pharaoh is willing to bargain with God (v. 10)?   3/ Contrast Moses and Pharaoh in their responsibilities to the agreement and their responses.   4/ In the plague of the gnats what indirect counsel does Pharaoh receive from his advisors? How do they recognize the power of God?   5/ Recall situations in which you have had a choice of listening to advisors and God or of becoming hardened to the voice of God. What has been your reaction in the situation?   6/ What is the new distinction in the plague of flies? Imagine the Israelites' feelings.   7/ How far does Pharaoh go in his bargaining now? Why doesn't Moses agree to the first concession? What further concession does Pharaoh make? What is Moses' warning to him?

DAY *15* △ *Exodus 9*

1/ Distinguish the twofold purpose of God in sending these catastrophes.   2/ On what basis is the plague of hail "selective"?   3/ What is Pharaoh's reaction this time? What does he admit? Do you think he is genuinely sorry for sin or remorseful because of the consequences?   4/ For what reasons is the plague stopped?   5/ What is the danger to you in not listening to God?   6/ What qualities of *a*—Pharaoh, *b*—Moses, and *c*—God are revealed by their actions here?

DAY *16* △ *Exodus 10*

1/ What additional insight does God give for all these signs?   2/To what extent do God's purposes take into account the Egyptians' attitude toward him?   3/ What is *a*—God's and *b*—Pharaoh's part in Pharaoh's hardened heart?   4/ How can you encourage others by telling what God has done?   5/ Imagine the pressure placed on Pharaoh by God and by Pharaoh's servants. What are the two points of view?   6/ How does the ninth plague affront the Egyptian sun god Ra?   7/ As events build toward the final battle, with Egypt a disaster area, for what truce terms does Pharaoh hold out (vv. 8-11, 24)?   8/ How has Pharaoh sinned against *a*—God and *b*—Moses and Aaron?   9/ Contrast the ultimate implications if Moses agrees to Pharaoh's terms or holds out for unconditional surrender (cf. 6:5-8).   10/ How many opportunities has God given Pharaoh to repent? Considering this what is different about the last catastrophe?

DAY *17* △ *Exodus 11—12:20*

1/ Account for the attitude of the Egyptians and Pharaoh's servants toward Moses and Israelites. What is one practical consequence of this attitude?   2/ Summarize God's description of his next strategic move against Pharaoh (death of the sacred animals is a major religious catastrophe). 3/ Single out the requirements of the lamb and how it is to be prepared and used for the initial celebration. 4/ What is the criterion for safety from this plague?  5/ What are additional instructions for the annual memorial? the consequences of disobedience?  6/ In what ways do you observe or remember what the Lord has done for you? How meaningful is this to you? Why?

DAY *18*  △  *Exodus 12:21–13:16*

1/ Add to your previous list of requirements for the passover celebration the additional instructions Moses gives the elders. What is the response of the people?  2/ Imagine the terror and anguish spreading from house to house.  3/ Contrast Pharoah's response now to his previous reactions. How do the Egyptians punctuate his command?  4/ Describe and imagine Egypt before and after God's acts of judgment.  5/ Summarize the contrasting responses of Moses and Pharaoh to God in these encounters. What is the basic issue that differentiates them?  6/ How do you respond to God's commandments? Why?  7/ Who and what constitute this emigration? Consider the effect of these facts on their speed in travel.  8/ Compare 12:40-42 and 13:3-10 with Genesis 15:13-16. List the specific fulfillments of God's promise (note in vv. 9, 16—phylacteries are rolled parchments inscribed with passages from the law, placed into small boxes and attached to Jewish males' wrist and put on the forehead during prayer).  9/ Who is unable to celebrate the annual passover feast. On what basis is this altered?  10/ What does the Lord demand regarding the firstborn? What provision does he make for the life of a firstborn son?  11/ In what specific ways can you put God first in considering possessions and family?

DAY *19*  △  *Exodus 13:17–14:31*

1/ Why doesn't God lead the people through a short cut?  2/ How are they to know their way through the desert without a road map?  3/ Follow their journey on a map (continue in subsequent days).  4/ With Egypt a disaster area and its labor force gone consider the logic and strategy in Pharaoh's next move.  5/ Describe your feelings were you an Israelite in this situation: surrounded by sea, desert, mountains, and an armed enemy.  6/ Contrast the reactions of a—the people and b—Moses.  7/ Trace the steps as God delivers Israel again.  8/ Describe and imagine the weather conditions as Israel crosses. Why is instant obedience essential?  9/ Contrast the reaction of *a*—the Egyptians and *b*—the Israelites to God's actions. 10/ What tough situations have you been in recently? Can you see God's design in these? What specifically have you learned today that can help you face hopeless situations? 11/ Contrast the Egyptians' end with the previous Pharaoh's intentions of 1:9-10.

DAY 20  △  *Exodus 15:1-21*

1/ Divide this folk song into appropriate stanzas and refrains. Summarize the thought of each. 2/ Describe God as to his character and his work as portrayed in the song. 3/ How is Moses' confidence for the future built on *a*—his knowledge of the character of God and *b*—his past experience? 4/ On what do you base your hope and plans for the future? 5/ How do you usually praise God freely? 6/ Write a song or verse praising God for what you have learned about him.

DAY 21  △  *Exodus 15:22—16:36*

1/ Imagine that you are one of this human mass. Recall the events of the previous days. How do you react in the face of the present situation? 2/ Differentiate the attitudes of *a*—the people and *b*—Moses at Marah. What is God's answer? 3/ What are the conditions of the promise God makes with the people? What right has he to ask so much? 4/ What is Israel's plight in the wilderness of Sin? Whom do they blame? Whom are they really griping against? 5/ When you complain about difficult circumstances, whom are you complaining against? 6/ What instructions accompany God's provision? 7/ Contrast the effects of obedience and disobedience to the detailed instructions. 8/ In what ways have you experienced the Lord's provision? What has been your response?

DAY 22  △  *Exodus 17*

1/ Compare this plight with those of 15:22-25 and 16:1-8 (type of test, reaction of Israel, reaction of the leaders, the answer). Is any progress evidenced? 2/ What point does Moses make clear in verse 2? What is his part in meeting the need? 3/ Describe Israel's first battle with an organized army. 4/ What part do each of the following have in the battle and victory: Joshua and the army? Moses? Aaron and Hur? 5/ What is the significance of God's new revelation to them? 6/ Account for the difference of character of *a*—Israel and *b*—Moses. With whom would you have to identify now?

7/ What are you learning from this study that can orient you in developing a right character and attitude toward God?

DAY 23    △    *Exodus 18*

1/ What is the leader Moses' attitude toward his father-in-law?    2/ List the areas of concern Moses covers in his report (v. 8).    3/ When and how have you recently given a spiritual progress report? Do you usually include both hardships and victory honestly?    4/ What is Jethro's response? What does he learn about God from this account?    5/ How have you been convinced of God's greatness? 6/ Imagine the disputes which arise among 600,000 men with their wives and families, uprooted from home traveling through the desert. How are these settled?    7/ What advice does Jethro give?    8/ What kind of men is Moses to choose?    9/ Differentiate the part of *a*—the assistants and *b*—Moses.    10/ Would you meet Jethro's qualifications?    11/ Why would you like men of similar quality over you?    12/ What responsibilities of yours have you delegated to others? Have you been gracious as Moses?

DAY 24    △    *Exodus 19*

1/ Contrast Israel's past status with God's future for them (the eagle flies beneath fledglings to support them if necessary).    2/ What is Israel's part in this agreement?    3/ How does God's goal for Israel relate to his statement *all the earth is mine*?    4/ What has God done for you?    5/ How do the people respond (v. 8)?    6/ What is God's next step? What is Moses' role in this?    7/ List the actions and precautions the people are to take when God speaks with Moses. 8/ Describe the scene the third day (note the positions of *a*—the people and *b*—Moses in relation to God). Imagine their feelings. 9/ What attributes of God's character are demonstrated in this chapter?    10/ Summarize God's activity in this chapter as to *a*— contact with people, *b*—the way he reveals himself, and *c*—the limitations he sets.

DAY 25    △    *Exodus 20*

1/ What right does God have to demand Israel's primary allegiance? 2/ List the next three commandments and God's reason for asking obedience to each (vv. 4-11). What aspect of God's being does each protect?    3/ How do you keep the sabbath day *holy*?    4/ With what relationship do verses 12-17 deal? Which ones concern personality? physical body? possessions? 5/ In what ways have you been thoughtless of the total well-being of parents and other people this week? 6/ How do the people react to this event? 7/ What reason does Moses give for God's action? 8/ What evidence do you see in your life that God is more eager to keep you from sin than you are to avoid it? 9/ Summarize what Israel learns of God's character and nature from this confrontation. 10/ How does this encounter enlarge or change your concept of God? 11/ What additional demands does he make concerning worship? 12/ Contrast the content of these commandments with the practices of the surrounding nations. 13/ Briefly summarize the content and principles of *Exodus* so far.

DAY 26  △  *Acts 13:1-3*
1/ Summarize the effects of church growth and the power of the Holy Spirit as related in the first twelve chapters. 2/ Describe the church at Antioch. How similar to this church is your Christian group? What do you do when you get together? What results? 3/ Distinguish the part of God and the part of the church in sending out missionaries. What principles regarding a missionary call do you derive from this? 4/ Is your ministry from the Holy Spirit or one you have thought up?

DAY 27  △  *Acts 13:4-12*
1/ Trace the travels of these men on a map (continue on subsequent days). 2/ How do Paul and his company make their initial contacts in each town? 3/ What do you do with obvious opportunities God gives you? What is your attitude toward telling others about Jesus? 4/ Find at least four evidences that the Holy Spirit is active in the incident with Sergius Paulus and Elymas (cf. the events of vv. 1-3). 5/ When have you been bold for God in a difficult situation? What has happened? How can you have more boldness?

DAY 28  △  *Acts 13:13-41*
1/ Visualize this situation. To whom is Paul speaking? How does his audience affect what he says and how he says it? 2/ Do you keep in mind your listeners' background when speaking of the gospel? 3/ List what this message teaches you about God (underline the verbs in vv. 17-23). 4/ What is the main point of Paul's

sermon? List what facts he gives about Jesus. 5/ What does Paul mean by *the good news* (v. 32)? Is your message to those about you good news to them? 6/ What is the content of your message: a living person or ethics, rules, and religious convictions? 7/ What place does God's word have in Paul's message? in yours?

DAY 29   △   *Acts 13:42-52*
1/ What are the initial results of Paul's witness in the synagogue at Antioch? What is the reaction to Paul's message a week later? Why? 2/ How do Paul and Barnabas answer those who are opposing them? 3/ When your gospel witness is reviled, are you justified in similar actions? 4/ Who decides who will believe the gospel message (v. 48)? How can this fact encourage you in your witness today? 5/ What different emotions does the gospel stir up in Antioch? In what ways are you prepared for these varying responses to your Christian witness?

DAY 30   △   *Acts 14:1-7*
1/ How is Paul's reception at Iconium similar to his reception at Antioch? What circumstances lead Paul to decide to remain a long time here? 2/ What is the source of the opposition? 3/ Summarize Paul's message (cf. v. 3—the word of God's grace) as presented in chapter 13. 4/ What specific help does God give Paul and Barnabas at Iconium? In what ways does the Lord *bear witness* to your message? 5/ How do the people of the city respond to the miraculous? 6/ At what point do Paul and Barnabas decide to leave Iconium? Where do they go? What do they do?

## MONTH 7

DAY 1   △   *Acts 14:8-28*
1/ How does Paul's approach at Lystra differ from his approach at Antioch and Iconium? 2/ Describe the religion of the people of Lystra. What do they learn about the one true God this day? 3/ What ideas of God are held by those around you? 4/ Contrast the attitudes of the people toward the apostles in *a*-verse 18 and *b*-verse 19. What does this reveal about the psychology of these people? 5/ How important is follow up to Paul? How does he counsel new Christians (v. 22)? To whom can you give this counsel today?

6/ How do Paul and Barnabas provide for the future needs of the believers in Lystra, Iconium, and Antioch (v. 23)? 7/ What is Paul's relation to the Antioch church which has sent them out (cf. 13:1-3)? What principles can you derive from this relationship as to how you and your Christian work should be related to a local church?

### DAY 2  △  Acts 15:1-21

1/ What is the issue that occasions this conference? Why is this such an important and controversial matter (esp. vv. 1, 5, 10-11)? 2/ Have you ever had a disagreement with anyone over what men must do to be saved? What position have you taken? 3/ How do the apostles and elders arrive at their conclusion? What can you learn from this about handling controversies among believers? 4/ To whom should a local church appeal when it cannot resolve its controversies? To whom does the church at Antioch appeal? 5/ What do the apostles and elders finally decide? 6/ When someone from a background very different from yours becomes a Christian, what do you expect of him? 7/ What do you consider essential to being a Christian? to Christian life and growth? What is the basis for your opinions?

### DAY 3  △  Acts 15:22-35

1/ How do the apostles and elders carry out their solution to the problem confronting Gentile believers (cf. v. 5)? How well do you implement your decisions? 2/ What kind of men are chosen to take the letter to Antioch? 3/ Does Jesus Christ mean more to you than your life? How do you know? 4/ How is the news received in Antioch? 5/ What are some "burdens" you lay on yourself and other Christians? In what ways have you drifted into a legalism that demands what God has not demanded? 6/ How can the kind of relationship between the churches at Antioch and Jerusalem be fostered in church relations today?

### DAY 4  △  Acts 15:36—16:5

1/ What causes sharp contention between Paul and Barnabas (cf. 13:13)? What happens? How does God overrule this argument for good? 2/ Why, do you think, do Paul and Barnabas choose to work with someone else rather than alone? Do you have a friend with whom you work, pray, and share God's workings? If not, can you ask God to give you such a person? 3/ How can you reconcile Paul's action regarding Timothy with the decision of the apostles and elders in chapter 15?

DAY 5  △  *Acts 16:6-10*

1/ What indicates that Luke probably joins Paul at this time? 2/ How is Paul guided to cross over from Asia into Europe with the gospel? 3/ In what ways does God guide you into the right places? Where does he want you today? 4/ What persons of the trinity are mentioned in these verses? What is said about each? 5/ What terms does Luke use in this passage to describe Paul's evangelistic work? Can your Christian testimony truthfully be described by these terms?

DAY 6  △  *Acts 16:11-24*

1/ What kind of place is Philippi? What light does this give to Paul's missionary strategy here? 2/ Contrast the various people the apostle encounters in this city. 3/ Why does Lydia believe Paul's message? 4/ Why do the owners of the slave girl oppose Paul? What charge do they bring against Paul and Silas (cf. with the events of vv. 16-18)? 5/ Contrast Paul's treatment in Philippi with the vision in verse 9. Does doing the will of God necessarily exclude trouble?

DAY 7  △  *Acts 16:25-40*

1/ How do Paul and Silas respond to the discouraging circumstances of verse 22-24? When you think God clearly leads you into a situation, and then everything goes wrong, how do you feel? 2/ Imagine the events of verse 26 taking place at your state penitentiary. What is the result? 3/ Contrast the outcome of Paul and Silas' remaining at the prison with the probable outcome of their escape (cf. esp. v. 28). 4/ How important, do you think, is their conduct in the jailer's conversion? 5/ What do these circumstances and results teach you about the ways of God? 6/ When has God worked in your life similarly to his work in Paul and Silas' experience? How can God advance the gospel through your troubles today? 7/ What encouragement can you find in today's passage (cf. v. 15; 2:39) concerning God's purposes for the unsaved members of your family? Are you praying regularly for those in your family who as yet are not Christians?  8/ What do verses 35-40 teach about a right concern for public reputation?

DAY 8  △  *Acts 17:1-15*

1/ Contrast the attitudes of the Jews in Thessalonica and Beroea toward Paul's teaching. What is his method of teaching? What is the result in both places (follow his correspondence in *1* and *2 Thessalonians*)?  2/ How will the example of the Jews in Beroea affect the frequency and method of your personal Bible study?  3/ What is the basis of your witness to non-Christians?  4/ Who incites opposition? Why?

DAY 9  △  *Acts 17:16-34*

1/What different kinds of people does Paul meet in Athens? What are their interests and beliefs (contrast the Epicurean and Stoic philosophies)?  2/ How does Paul begin his missionary work in this city?  3/ In his sermon at the Areopagus how does Paul move step by step from the Athenian idols to Jesus Christ? What does Paul tell the Athenians that God wants them to do?  4/ At what point and in what ways does Paul's message conflict with Epicurean and Stoic beliefs?  5/ What are common philosophies of life around you? In what ways does the Christian message differ from these? 6/ How much stress do you place on repentance and future judgment in your Christian witness?  7/ What is the result of the message of Christ in Athens?

DAY 10  △  *Acts 18:1-11*

1/ How does God lead Paul in Corinth with regard to housing, activity, and length of stay? What does this teach you about God? about Paul? Do you seek God's guidance in these areas?  2/ What significant change in strategy does Paul make when the Jews of the synagogue oppose his message? What do you do when you meet with continual opposition to the gospel from certain groups?  3/ What does God's counsel to Paul (vv. 9-10) indicate about Paul's feelings toward remaining in Corinth (follow his correspondence in *1* and *2 Corinthians*)  4/ In what ways have you experienced God's protection from opposition? What kind of situation are you in now: much response or little response? How do you know?

71

DAY *11*  △  *Acts 18:12-28*

1/ Of what do the Jews accuse Paul? What is Gallio's response?  2/ Describe Gallio's attitudes and actions as a civil ruler in this instance. Do you think that government officials today should try to decide religious controversies?  3/ How much ground does Paul cover here (keep checking Paul's travels on a map)?  4/ What conditions does Paul place on his promise to return to Ephesus? What does this reveal about Paul's concept of God? What about your concept of God do your plans and promises reveal?  5/ What gifts does Apollos have? How is he using them? What is missing in his knowledge of the Christian message?  6/ What ministry do Priscilla and Aquila have to Apollos? What does this interaction reveal about the early Christians (compare or contrast with your interactions with other Christians today)?  7/ In what situations are you open and teachable from the Lord? from other Christians?  8/ What does Apollos do with his new knowledge? What do you do with the enlarged understanding you receive about God?

DAY *12*  △  *Acts 19:1-10*

1/ Compare the situation of the twelve disciples at Ephesus with Apollos' situation in 18:24-26. How does Paul explain the true significance of John's baptism (cf. Luke 3:3-17)? How do these men show their faith in Jesus?  2/ What evidence is in your life that you have been *baptized* by the Holy Spirit?  3/ What is Paul's reaction to stubbornness, disbelief, and slander?  4/ What is the time span involved?  5/ What steps are you taking now to bring about a situation in your community similar to verse 10?

DAY *13*  △  *Acts 19:11-22*

1/ What extraordinary results does God produce in Ephesus? Why, do you think, does he work in this way (cf. the superstition, magical practices, and worship of the moon goddess Diana in Ephesus)?  2/ Of what significance is the incident of verses 14-17 to *a*-the exorcists and *b*-the people? What does this incident reveal about *a*-Satan and *b*-God?  3/ What are some modern counterparts of the Ephesian superstition and magic?  4/ What difference does being a Christian make in your practices? In what ways can God use you to rout basic evils in the culture in which he places you?  5/ What long-range planning does Paul make in verses 21-22 (follow the unusual circumstances and delays he encounters in the rest of Acts)? What intermediate steps does he take? 6/ What long-range plans do you have for your Christian service? What steps will you need to take to fulfill those plans?

DAY *14* △ *Acts 19:23-41*

1/ What causes the new wave of opposition? What brings it to an end? 2/ Describe the crowd as to their a-zeal for the moon goddess Diana (Artemis), b-confusion, c-impulsiveness, and d-prejudice. Are they different from people you know? 3/ What does this incident reveal about the results of the gospel in society? What observable changes have resulted from the gospel where you have been?

DAY *15* △ *Acts 20:1-12*

1/ Imagine the fellowship of these Christians traveling together. Where do they go? What do they talk about? pray about? share of fears and joys? 2/ Describe the attitude of the church at Troas toward learning more about the Lord. 3/ In what ways does the occupation of Luke bear on the a-veracity and b-inclusion of the incident concerning Eutychus? 4/ Imagine the physical strain of Paul's ministry (cf. previous chaps.). 5/ In what ways do you take advantage of the opportunities God gives you for spiritual growth (even when it causes you personal inconvenience)?

DAY *16* △ *Acts 20:13-38*

1/ Try to capture the vivid picture Paul gives here of his service for Jesus Christ. What does this service involve in terms of his a-motivation, b-message, c-methods, d-self image, e-trials, and f-relationships with people? To what degree is this an accurate description of your service for the Lord? 2/ What can you learn from this passage about the government of a local church? 3/ To what dangers is a local church exposed? What safeguards does Paul present? What are the responsibilities of the elders? 4/How is Paul supported in Ephesus (cf. 18:3; 28:30)? What is his reason? 5/ What is the elders' response to Paul?

DAY *17* △ *Acts 21:1-6*

1/ What initiative does Paul take at Tyre? 2/ In what ways and for what reasons do you actively seek out other Christians at the place where you work? in your neighborhood? on your campus? 3/ Compare this beach incident with 20:36-37. What qualities of fellowship are revealed? Characterize your relationship with other Christians.

DAY *18*  △  *Acts 21:7-16*

1/ How do Paul's friends feel about his going to Jerusalem? Why? 2/ What is Paul's conviction? Why (cf. 19:21; 20:22-24)? 3/ When the advice of Christian friends conflicts with your own conviction, what do you do? 4/ What differing views of suffering and trouble are reflected in this passage? When and in what kind of situations do you usually take the easy way out to bypass unpleasantness?

DAY *19*  △  *Acts 21:17-39*

1/ Imagine the growth of the Jerusalem church during the intervening years. What conflict still exists (cf. 15:4-35)? 2/ What results when Paul relates God's workings to the brethren in Jerusalem? What kind of happenings do you share with Christian friends? 3/ What problem do the elders anticipate by Paul's presence in Jerusalem? What counsel do they give (cf. Num. 6:13-21)? What is Paul's response? 4/ Without compromising principle how do you accommodate yourself to the attitudes and convictions of other Christians? 5/ What danger befalls Paul when he takes the advice of the elders (cf. the charge against Stephen in 6:8-15)? What means does God use to save Paul's life?

DAY *20*  △  *Acts 21:40—22:29*

1/ Imagine the scene and tension (cf. 21:27-39). Why, do you think, does Paul want to address this crowd instead of accepting the safety of the barracks? 2/ What is the *a*-content and *b*-basis of Paul's defense? What can you learn from this defense about giving a testimony? 3/ How does the crowd respond to Paul's speech? What about their attitudes does the crowd's response reveal? 4/ What are modern counterparts of this situation? 5/ In what situations do you *a*-relate the whole truth of God's message and *b*-leave out unpopular truths in the face of antagonistic opinion? What are the consequences in each situation?

DAY *21*  △  *Acts 22:30—23:11*

1/ How does Paul show his willingness to submit to the scriptures? 2/ When do you judge your conduct by the Word of God (even when those around you are flagrantly violating it)? 3/ How do the Pharisees and Sadducees differ theologically? What is Paul's strategy in raising the question of the resurrection of the dead? 4/ Imagine the uproar of the council. 5/ What special encouragement does God give Paul at this time? In what times of need have you been encouraged by God?

DAY 22  △  *Acts 23:12-35*
1/ How does God rescue Paul from the guerrilla attempt to kill him? 2/ Characterize Paul's nephew. Imagine the family concern for Paul. 3/ What does this incident reveal about a-Paul's reputation, b-the Roman government, and c-God's work in the world? 4/ What is the basis of your confidence amidst turmoil and unrest?

DAY 23  △  *Acts 24:1-27*
1/ List the specific accusations against Paul (cf. v. 5 with v. 2)? 2/ What is Paul's defense? How does he answer each charge? 3/ What is the core of the problem according to Paul? 4/ What concept of Christianity do those around you have from what you a-tell them and b-indicate by your attitude and conduct? 5/ Characterize Felix. What are his responses? his motives?

DAY 24  △  *Acts 25:1-22*
1/ What kind of person is Festus? What fault do Felix and Festus have in common? 2/ What kind of influence is Paul having on the authorities (cf. 9:15-16)? 3/ What are Paul's views of justice? What are yours? 4/ What is the movement toward Rome here? How does Festus present Paul's case to Agrippa? 5/ Imagine you are Paul. What are your feelings now?

DAY 25  △  *Acts 25:23—26:32*
1/ Imagine the contents of Festus' letter to Caesar. 2/ Picture this situation. What is the source of Paul's courage (cf. 23:11)? 2/ Characterize Paul's early life. To what does he ascribe the revolutionary change in his life? 3/ According to Paul what is the real issue of his defense? 4/ What has been your response to your knowledge of God? 5/ Compare the responses of Festus and Agrippa. 6/ In what ways has your knowing God been worth what it has *cost* you?

DAY *26* △ *Acts 27:1-44*

1/ With whom does Paul sail (follow the trip on a map)? 2/ Imagine the weather conditions and frantic measures to keep afloat. 3/ Contrast the reactions of a-Paul and b-those on board throughout this chapter. What do their reactions show about them? 4/ What kind of influence does Paul have on the ship? Why, do you think? 5/ What do these events reveal about God (esp. vv. 23-24)? 6/ What do your reactions in times of stress and difficulty reveal about your faith in God's control of every situation? How do your reactions affect others?

DAY *27* △ *Acts 28:1-10*

1/ How does God continue to manifest his sovereignty? 2/ Describe Paul's action and character here. In what ways do you try to be observant and helpful in your immediate situations? 3/ Through what means does God provide opportunities for service in Malta? How does Paul serve others here? Imagine Paul's feelings. 4/ What a-everyday or occasional contacts and b-time do you consider useless or lacking in potential for service opportunities? In what ways can you change this attitude today?

DAY *28* △ *Acts 28:11-22*

1/ Imagine yourself in Paul's situation. What are your feelings as you dock (cf. 19:21)? 2/ What does Paul do when he arrives? 3/ How does Paul's arrival in Rome demonstrate God's faithfulness (cf. 23:11)? Do you really believe that God keeps his promises? What promises are especially relevant to your needs today? 4/ What kind of response does Paul receive from the Jews in Rome? Characterize these Jews.

DAY *29* △ *Acts 28:23-31*

1/ What is Paul's message to the Jews in Rome? What is his authority as he preaches? 2/ In what ways is their response typical? 3/ What does the passage quoted from Isaiah teach about the nature of man? Why don't people understand God's message? 4/ What should you do when your friends and neighbors don't understand? 5/ What does Paul do now that he is living in Rome?

DAY *30* △ *Acts 13–28*

1/ Summarize what Paul accomplishes on each of his missionary journeys. 2/ What types of *a*-people and *b*-problems does he encounter? What is his influence on the people? How does he deal with the problems? 3/ Summarize the Jewish-Gentile controversy. What are Paul's views (follow his arguments in *Galatians*)? 4/ Describe Paul's method of teaching and policy of follow up. 5/ Describe Christianity as presented here. Compare or contrast your belief and experience.

## MONTH 8

### DAY *1* △ Introduction to Amos
Amos is from Judah (the southern kingdom) but prophesies to Israel (the northern kingdom) during the reign of Jeroboam II. Israel is very prosperous but morally decadent. *Amos 1:1—2:5* 1/ Pinpoint on a map the seven nations (or their capitals) to which God speaks words of judgment. 2/ List the sins evoking God's judgment. What do they have in common? 3/ Imagine the people's feelings when they hear the doom of the surrounding nations. 4/ What is Judah's sin? How is it different from that of the other nations? 5/ At what point are you rejecting God's law for your life? Are you building your life on lies? 6/ How can you see yourself in God's perspective?

### DAY *2* △ Amos 2:6-16
1/ How does God's judgment now become personal? Why will God punish Israel (cf. v. 8 with Ex. 22:26)? Categorize their sins. 2/ How does Israel's sin profane God's name? How does yours? 3/ What are three specific things God has done for Israel? 4/ How has Israel welcomed God's men (Nazarites) sent to them? How do you respond to God's messengers today (even if their message exposes your sin)? 5/ What inevitable consequences follow when a person or group turn away from God?

### DAY *3* △ Amos 3
1/ What relationship does God have with Israel? 2/ How does Amos justify his prophesying? 3/ What does God do before he acts in judgment? 4/ How do you feel when your sin is exposed in front of people you want to impress? 5/ How will God bring judgment? Describe its extent. 6/ What do the closing verses

suggest about the affluence and materialism of Israel (cf. 6:4-7)?
7/ What will happen to a-Israel's and b-your material possessions?

DAY *4*  △  *Amos 4*

1/ In addition to the destruction of their cities and homes what
will happen to the people of Israel because of their sin?  2/ To
whom does *cows of Bashan* refer? Imagine your reaction to this description.  3/ What is ironical about the people's actions and God's
attitude toward them in verses 4-5? What are you trying to accomplish through your religious activities?  4/ How has God warned
Israel before its final destruction? What does this reveal about God's
attitude toward his people?  5/ If they refuse the early warnings,
what must they face?  6/ What are God's feelings about punishment and judgment?  7/ What qualities of God's character are
evident from this passage?  8/ How are his character and acts
related?

DAY *5*  △  *Amos 5–6*

1/ What two manifestations of God's nature are seen in 5:1-15?
How are they related?  2/ List and explain Israel's sins. What will
be the consequences (esp. 5:16, 27; 6:7)?  3/ Contrast Israel's
feelings of safety and confidence with these consequences.  4/
what makes God hate the religious activities of his people?  5/
What does he want in their lives? How can you show these qualities
in your life today?

DAY *6*  △  *Amos 7*

1/ What three visions are given to Amos in verses 1-9? Distinguish
their types of destruction.  2/ How does God respond to Amos'
pleas for mercy? What do these actions reveal about a-Amos' and
b-God's character?  3/ What charge does Amaziah the priest bring
against Amos? How does Amos answer the charge? Contrast a-
Amaziah's and b-God's instructions to Amos.  4/ Imagine the
priest's reaction to Amos' prophecy regarding him.  5/ Why is
God's messenger and message not always cordially welcome in
society (even among religious leaders)? Whom do you usually
heed—God's message and messenger or accepted (but doctrinally
questionable) religious leaders? Why?

DAY 7   △   *Amos 8*

1/What does the vision of summer fruit (which is over-ripe, spoiling) illustrate? What will change?   2/ What motives prompt the sins of verses 4-6?   3/ What kind of famine is predicted in verses 11-12? Is the word of God daily food to your life? What difference would a similar famine today make in your life?   4/ How have you been nourished by the study of *Amos?*

DAY 8   △   *Amos 9*

1/ What is Amos' final vision? What does this vision reveal about the judgment of God?   2/ What will happen after the forthcoming judgment (vv. 11-15)?   3/ What is your hope beyond the destructions of this life? How does your conduct show that you have a hope? 4/ What is revealed in this book about the character of God?   5/ Briefly characterize Amos. Summarize his message. What metaphors does he use to convey his message?   6/ Briefly summarize the moral, socio-economic, and political situation of Israel here.

DAY 9   △   *Introduction to Hosea*

Hosea prophesies from the end of Jeroboam II's rule (741) to 701. The kingdoms of Israel and Judah are divided. He speaks primarily to Israel. The book mirrors the political, social, and religious condition of Israel at the time. *Hosea 1*   1/ List the ways in which Hosea's domestic life portrays the life of the nation of Israel.   2/ How are the children's names significant (cf. 2 Kings 10)? What progression is sketched by the meaning of these names?   3/ What image is portrayed by the last paragraph? What relation do verses 10-11 have to verses 4-8? How can these contrasting images come from the same person?

DAY 10   △   *Hosea 2:1-13*

1/ Make two columns (Hosea—Gomer and God—Israel) to compare Hosea's married life with the life of Israel under God.   2/ Imagine Hosea's (God's) feelings about the developments in his marriage. Why doesn't he plead with Gomer (Israel) directly?   3/ What is his version of the reasons she leaves him?   4/ What action does he plan to take?   5/ In what ways are you like Gomer?   6/ How has God made you realize that life's good things are from him?

DAY *11*  △  *Hosea 2:14-23*

1/ How is this section connected with verses 1-13?   2/ List God's acts of restoration. What is his objective in this restoration?   3/ List the characteristics of God's betrothal.   4/ In what way has God "courted" you? What are the characteristics of your betrothal relationship? How do you handle other suitors?

DAY *12*  △  *Hosea 3—4*

1/ What has happened to Gomer? What is involved before Hosea can live with her again?   2/ How does this reunion depict God's relationship with Israel? with you?   3/ What indictment does God make about Israel (Ephraim means Israel here)? What is the extended effect of sin?   4/ How does God diagnose the cause of this plight?   5/ How are the people's sins related to the priests' sins?   6/ Define *knowledge*. What are you doing to acquire this knowledge?

DAY *13*  △  *Hosea 5—6*

1/ List the charges God brings against Israel? What imagery does he use?   2/ What responsibility do the leaders have for the spiritual decline?   3/ List the consequences of their sins.   4/ How is God's judgment rehabilitative?   5/ How does Ephraim react to God's judgment?   6/ How are you like Ephraim? What can you learn from their mistakes?   7/ What does this passage reveal about God?   8/ How can you guard against superficial response to God?

DAY *14*  △  *Hosea 7—8*

1/ List the metaphors describing Israel. What do they reveal?   2/ What is God's attitude toward Israel?   3/ Why hasn't Israel turned to him for forgiveness? Account for their blindness.   4/ How do you guard against blindness to sin?

DAY *15*  △  *Hosea 9*

1/ What forms will God's judgment take? How will the people be affected?   2/ Why does God do this?   3/ How are God's love and his judgment related?   4/ What do you learn about the seriousness of sin? What is your attitude toward sin?

DAY *16*  △  *Hosea 10*

1/ Describe the reaction of Israel to each of the following national conditions: prosperity, loss of their king, destruction of their idols, military might.   2/ Why do affluence and military prowess pose threats for the people of God?   3/ How much of your life is aimed at achieving security?   4/ Can God trust you with affluence?

#### DAY 17   △   Hosea 11–12

1/ List the actions of God toward the people. How do they respond? 2/ Describe God's feelings toward them. What confidence does this knowledge of God give to you?   3/ Describe God as judge. Why is his judgment vindictive?   4/ How should this knowledge of God affect your acts of confession of sin?

#### DAY 18   △   Hosea 13

1/ How is Israel described?   2/ Trace the spiritual decline.   3/ Why do they defect?   4/ Why doesn't God offer them another chance?   5/ What are the warnings for you through Israel's example? What are the errors to avoid?

#### DAY 19   △   Hosea 14

1/ What have you expected to read in the last chapter of this book? 2/ What are some characteristics of the repentance to which Hosea calls Israel?   3/ Why does repentance involve specifics as in verse 3?   4/ What is the cause and effect relationship in repentance? Why do men hesitate to return to God in repentance? Why do you? 5/ Resketch the manner in which Hosea's life with Gomer is a reflection of God's relationship with Israel. How do the children's names (and new names) portray the content of the entire book?

#### DAY 20   △   Psalm 13

1/ How many times are first person pronouns used in this psalm? What does this reveal?   2/ What seems to be the psalmist's problem?   3/ For what reasons is he sorrowful?   4/ What does he ask God to do? Why?   5/ Contrast verses 1-2 with verses 5-6. What is the difference in the mood of the psalmist?   6/ What three things characterize David in these two closing verses? What three things characterize God? To what extent can you identify with verses 5-6? 7/ Title this psalm as to content.

#### DAY 21   △   Psalm 14

1/ What kind of person says "There is no God"? How does God re-

gard such a person?   2/ What effects are produced in daily living
by this kind of attitude toward God?   3/ What moral standards is
God looking for? What does he find?   4/ Define *refuge*. For whom
is God a *refuge?*   5/ What does *no knowledge of God* produce?
How has your knowledge of God deepened recently?   6/ What is
the effect of the injustice and corruption on David? What is his hope?
7/ How much of the fool's unauthoritative principle of living in this
psalm fits your experience?   8/ Title this psalm as to content.

### DAY 22   △   *Psalm 15*

1/ What relationship is pictured in verse 1?   2/ List and explain
the qualifications for the person who wants to live in fellowship with
God? How can these be real in your life?   3/ What areas of human
experience are included in this list?   4/ What is the godly man's
goal? What is his attitude toward himself? toward others?   5/ By
what single standard does the man who pleases God judge others?
6/ How do you score on this check-list? Where are your problem
areas? What are you going to do about them? when?   7/ Title this
psalm as to content.

### DAY 23   △   *Psalm 16*

1/ What is the opening petition? Why is David hopeful?   2/ With
whom does David identify? Why?   3/ What attitudes does he express toward fellow believers? toward the ungodly?   4/ List and
meditate on what he says God does for or means to him. How many
of these do you find real in your life?   5/ What kind of God does
David know and trust? What expressions of assurance grow out of
this knowledge?   6/ On what note does this psalm close? Why?
7/ What threefold progression of mood and thought is revealed in
the psalm?   8/ How does trusting God like this affect you?   9/
Title this psalm as to content.

### DAY 24   △   *Psalm 17*

1/ In this prayer distinguish and title David's petitions (vv. 1-5,
6-12, 13-15). What is the basis of each petition?   2/ How does
David describe himself to the Lord? How does he describe God?
the wicked?   3/ What are the contrasting goals of himself and his
enemies?   4/ What does David ask God to do (vv. 13-14)?   5/
Contrast this petition with verse 15. What does this reveal about

David?    6/ How much of verses 1-5 can you make your prayer? How does your assurance compare with David's in verse 15?    7/ Title this psalm as to content.

### DAY 25  △  Psalm 18:1-24

1/ What is David's trial (cf. vv. 1-6 with 2 Samuel 22:1-51)?    2/ What things are said of God? To what extent have you found these descriptions true in your experience?    3/ What chief characteristic of God is set forth in verses 7-15? Explain the imagery. How do you describe the characteristic? in your viewpoint is it positive or negative? Why?    4/ In what ways has your experience paralleled the description of God in verses 16-19?    5/ As a rewarder how does God act? For what reasons does God deliver David? In what ways can you identify with David here?

### DAY 26  △  Psalm 18:25-50

1/ How is the justness of God shown in verses 25-30? What is your part in the way God acts toward you?    2/ What qualities does God honor in the man who prays?    3/ List the ways in which God is described as an enabler in verses 31-45. Which thought in this section is most important to you personally? Why?    4/ What physical advantages does David have? What does he credit as the source of these advantages?    5/ What does David emphasize in verses 46-50? How much of this are you prepared to claim as your experience today? in the days ahead?    6/ Title this psalm as to content (cf. vv. 1-24).

### DAY 27  △  Psalm 19

1/ What are two sources by which man can receive the knowledge of God?    2/ What aspects of creation are mentioned in verses 1-6? What is David attempting to point out here?    3/ How many things *of the Lord* are listed in verses 7-10? Where are they all found? Summarize their purpose.    4/ What is more important than wealth or luxuries?    5/ In verses 11-13 what is David's chief concern?    6/ What three types of sins are mentioned in these verses? Which of these do you currently practice? What can you do today to change that situation?    7/ What are the two aspects of the prayer in verse 14? How can you make it your prayer now?    8/ Title this psalm as to content.

DAY *28*  △  *Psalms 20–21*

1/ What type of situation prompts these psalms?  2/ List the words which show God's positive relationship with the people and king.  3/ What things does David desire? How does he express this desire (cf. 20:4 with 21:2)?  4/ In what ways does God *bless* the king (20:1-7)?  5/ Contrast David's and his enemies' confidence. What is the outcome of each?  6/ How does God deal with his enemies?  7/ In Psalm 21 how does verse 13 relate to verse 1? What is the significance of this relationship?  8/ What do you do when surrounded by trouble? Who is at the center of your plans?  9/ How do you go about getting *victory* in various situations? How does this compare with David's way? What is your response to *victory?*  10/ Title these psalms as to content.

DAY *29*  △  *Psalm 22*

1/ What emotional and physical experience prompt the expression of verses 1-2?  2/ What moods of the psalmist are evident?  3/ What is the basis for his belief in God?  4/ Is this psalm primarily negative or positive? Why?  5/ Contrast the beginning and ending. What makes the difference?  6/ What evidences do you find that this psalm has more than only immediate implications?  7/ At what points does this psalm depict your experiences? How?  8/ Title this psalm as to content.

DAY *30*  △  *Psalm 23*

1/ Characterize God as a shepherd and host. What areas of life's need are cared for by the shepherd?  2/ What phrases reveal David's attitudes toward God?  3/ What is significant about the use of pronouns?  4/ What is happening in verse 4 when David shifts to direct address?  5/ What time elements are present? What is their significance?  6/ Contrast the *a*-rest and activity, *b*-fear and comfort, *c*-danger and security, and *d*-want and provision. What do these contrasts reveal about God and man? How do they apply in your life?  7/ In what ways is the Lord your shepherd?  8/ Title this psalm as to content.

## MONTH 9

DAY *1*  △  *Psalm 24*

1/ To what extent is God sovereign? Why?  2/ What is the essential question in verse 3 (relate to the characteristics of God in vv. 1-2)?    3/ What standards are included in answer to that question? 4/ What is the historic and spiritual significance of verses 7-10?    5/ What is the major thrust of this psalm? Title the psalm.    6/ Where does this psalm affect you most penetratingly? Why?    7/ Who is the *King of glory?* How do you know?

### DAY 2 △ *Psalm 25*

1/ List the references which show David's dependence on God. How does his dependence relate to God's guidance?    2/ To what qualities of God's character does David appeal?    3/ What does God do for the humble? for the obedient? Why?    4/ In which category does David place himself? On what basis does he ask for pardon?    5/ In verses 11-15 what do you learn about the man who fears God?    6/ Summarize the thought in verses 12-14 and contrast with David's picture of his own need in verses 16-21.    7/ Which of David's words are familiar to your experience?    8/ What requests does David make of God in the closing verses? Which of these do you consider most important? Why?    9/ Title this psalm as to content.

### DAY 3 △ *Psalm 26*

1/ What is the dominant theme of this psalm? List the phrases that relate specifically to this theme.    2/ What picture of David is revealed here? What areas of his life does he include in his defense? What indicates his recognition of sin and guilt?    3/ How does David describe the wicked?    4/ What actions and attitudes should characterize a man of God? In how many of these can you honestly insert your name?    5/ How can you maintain *integrity* in an evil society?    6/ Title this psalm as to content.

### DAY 4 △ *Psalm 27*

1/ What do you learn about fear from this psalm?    2/ In what ways is the Lord your *a-light, b-salvation,* and *c-stronghold?*    3/ What is the singular desire of David? What do you want more than anything else this year?    4/ Why does David say he will *sing and make melody to the Lord?*    5/ Relate verses 7-10 with verse 4. What is the relationship of verses 11-12 with verses 1-3?    6/ Explain David's optimism in verse 13. What is the relationship between *seeing* and *believing* in the Christian life?    7/ What is David's *a-*

admonition and *b*-hope? What do these reveal about his view of God and man?   8/ What have you experienced to verify this relationship?   9/ Title this psalm as to content.

### DAY 5  △  *Psalm 28*
1/ What problem does David bring before God?   2/ Why is he so fervent in presenting this problem to God? When do you feel that God is silent—neither listening nor responding to you?   3/ Compare your problems to those David describes. How does David indicate his prayer has been answered?   4/ How has God *heard your voice?* Can you make verses 6-7 your own prayer?   5/ In what ways is the Lord your *a-strength, b-refuge,* and *c-shepherd?*   6/ Title this psalm as to content.

### DAY 6  △  *Psalm 29*
1/ Rephrase verses 1-2 so that they constitute a definition of worship. 2/ Trace the course of the storm (vv. 3-9). What qualities of God are revealed in the storm and its aftermath?   3/ Recreate imaginatively the whole picture presented in this psalm.   4/ How does the psalm help you *ascribe to the Lord glory and strength?*   5/ Title this psalm as to content.

### DAY 7  △  *Introduction to 1 Thessalonians*
Paul has sent Timothy to bring him reports about the new Christians he has abruptly left (cf. Acts 17:1-9) in Thessalonica. In response to Timothy's news Paul writes this letter to encourage the converts and complete his teaching of Christ's return. *1 Thessalonians 1*   1/ What are the evidences that God has worked in the lives of the Thessalonians? What similar evidences (or lack of them) are in your life?   2/ What specific areas of your relationship with people and with God are you able to describe with *work of faith, labor of love,* and *steadfastness of hope?*   3/ Describe Paul's presentation of the gospel and follow up.   4/ How do the Thessalonians and other people in the area hear about Jesus Christ (compare or contrast with the way people on your campus and in your neighborhood hear about him)?

### DAY 8  △  *1 Thessalonians 2:1-16*
1/ List the charges brought against Paul, Silas, and Timothy. How does Paul defend himself and his companions?   2/ What is their

attitude toward preaching the gospel? What is yours?   3/ Characterize the persecuting Jews.   4/ How can Paul and the others preach with joy and perseverance in the face of this persecution (v. 4)? How can you?   5/ What characteristics do Paul and the others show as they work with these new Christians?   6/ What characteristics of your life tend to prevent you from helping young Christians in such a way?

DAY 9   △   *1 Thessalonians 2:17—3:12*

1/ For what reasons is Timothy sent to visit the Thessalonian Christians?   2/ How have the Thessalonians responded to affliction? How have you?   3/ What indications of Paul's concern for them do they receive in this chapter?   4/ What ideas do you see in this chapter about how you can encourage other Christians (esp. those who are away from you)?   5/ What requests does Paul make of God for the Thessalonians?   6/Who are two Christians you can begin to pray for in this way?

DAY 10   △   *1 Thessalonians 4*

1/ What specific instructions does Paul give about God's will? What areas of life are involved?   2/ Which happenings in your life right now (and planned for the future) are in accordance with God's will? Which are not?   3/ How are the Thessalonians to express dynamically their love for others?   4/ How have you experienced God's teaching you to love other Christians recently?   5/ How are *holiness* and *love* related?   6/ What two reasons does Paul give for clarifying the second coming of Christ (vv. 13, 18)? 7/ What will happen to Christians who have died (*fallen asleep*) before Christ returns? those who are alive at the time?   8/ How does Paul substantiate these statements?   9/ Why are these facts an encouragement to you?

DAY 11   △   *1 Thessalonians 5*

1/ How is Christ's return unexpected? imminent?   2/ How are *a*-the Thessalonians and *b*-you to live in the meantime?   3/ Characterize and contrast people of *a-light* and *b-darkness*.   4/ Differentiate the three meanings of *sleep* in verses 1-10.   5/ List Paul's specific directions about responsibility to *a*-others and *b*-God.   6/ How does he remind them of the way in which a Christian be-

87

comes holy (vv. 23-24)?    7/ In what instances can you see this
taking place in your life?

DAY *12*    △    *Introduction to 2 Thessalonians*
In the face of additional misunderstanding Paul clarifies further his.
teaching about the second coming of Christ. *2 Thessalonians 1*    1/
Why does Paul thank God for the Thessalonians? What in their lives
causes Paul to boast about them?    2/ Can anyone observe these
things in your life?    3/ To what end does Paul always pray for
the Thessalonians? What connection does this prayer have with
Christ's return?    4/ Which concerns you most: your growth in
Christ or Christ's return to judge the unbeliever? Why? How does
this concern affect the way you live?    5/ Contrast the *a*-present
and *b*-future final situation of those who *a*-know and *b*-do not know
God.    6/ Compare and contrast *a*-Paul's style of writing and *b*-the
content of this chapter with the first of *1 Thessalonians*.

DAY *13*    △    *2 Thessalonians 2:1-12*
1/ What warning does Paul give the Thessalonians regarding
Christ's return? In what ways can you be similarly deceived?    2/
What happenings and attitudes will preceed Christ's return?    3/
Which of these seem to be fulfilled in the Roman Empire? Which
seem to be fulfilled today?    4/ How will Jesus' coming *destroy* the
*man of lawlessness?*    5/ On what basis will people be condemned?
6/ How will you express the truth today?

DAY *14*    △    *2 Thessalonians 2:13–3:5*
1/ Who are responsible for the Thessalonians' belief? In what ways?
List what each has done and will do for the Thessalonians.    2/
What direction does Paul want the Thessalonians to take in their
faith? On what basis?    3/ On what do you base your faith and
belief?

DAY *15*    △    *2 Thessalonians 3:6-17*
1/ What problem is discussed here?    2/ What part does jumping
to conclusions about Christ's return have in this problem?    3/
What kind of example are you for others?    4/ How does Paul
recommend treating a disobedient Christian?    5/ How does the
Lord's peace help you in the Christian community?    6/ Summarize

what you have learned from 1 and 2 Thessalonians about *a*-Christ's
return and *b*-life in the meantime.

### DAY *16* △ Introduction to Joshua

God chooses Joshua to assume the responsibility which has been
Moses'—to lead the Israelites into the promised land of Canaan (cf.
Gen. 35:9-12; Deut. 3:23-28; 34:1-9). *Joshua 1* 1/ What promises
does God give to Joshua concerning himself? concerning the people
of Israel? 2/ What commands does God give Joshua? What does
God stress about his law? 3/ What do you learn here about the
relationship between obedience and success? about the importance
of learning scripture? 4/ Contrast the contemporary view of success with the kind of success promised here. 5/ How does Joshua
respond to God's commission? On what basis does he deal with the
two and a half tribes (cf. Num. 32:1-32)? 6/ On what condition
do the people pledge obedience to Joshua? What fact about Moses
is stressed here and throughout the chapter? 7/ How does God's
promise to Joshua in verses 5 and 9 apply in your life today? In what
situations?

### DAY *17* △ Joshua 2

1/ Why, do you think, does Joshua send the spies to Jericho? What
does this show about Joshua? 2/ What risk does Rahab take in
hiding the spies? On what facts does she base her actions? 3/ How
does this chapter demonstrate that she acts in faith (esp. v. 11)?
4/ How are facts and faith related in your life? 5/ How does
Rahab's faith affect the spies? 6/ How do you expect to see God
going before you as he has for Israel?

### DAY *18* △ Joshua 3

1/ Imagine the thoughts and conversations of the Israelites during
the three days encampment by the Jordan River. Imagine you are
one of them. How do you feel in this situation? 2/ When does God
tell Joshua how the people will cross the river? 3/ What do you
learn here about acting and trusting God? 4/ What three things
will the people learn from this miracle? What phrase describes the
Lord? How is it significant here? 5/ What do you learn about God's
promises from this chapter?

DAY *19* △ *Joshua 4*

1/ What is the importance of the stone memorials? 2/ When faced with difficulty do you remember what God has done for you in past situations? 3/ How are the day's events significant for Joshua (cf. 1:5; 3:7)? 4/ How do the people go across the river (cf. v. 10)? Imagine the procession. 5/ What is the significance of the presence of the ark of the covenant? 6/ What does the timing in verse 18 indicate about the crossing (cf. v. 23)?

DAY *20* △ *Joshua 5*

1/ How does the news of God's actions (chap. 4) affect the surrounding peoples? 2/ For what reason does God command the renewal of circumcision (cf. Gen. 17:1-4; Ex. 12:48)? 3/ In what ways does this temporary disablement seem foolish? How has God prepared the way for it? What do you learn from Joshua at this point? 4/ What about your character is revealed by your response to all of God's commands? 5/ What does the celebration of the passover, the celebration of the feast of unleavened bread, and the cessation of manna mean to Israel at this time? 6/ How is the man (v. 13) related to the Israelites? How does Joshua respond to him?

DAY *21* △ *Joshua 6*

1/ What is God's promise to Joshua concerning Jericho? Locate this (and subsequent cities) on a map. 2/ Imagine yourself as *a*-Joshua, *b*-a watching soldier on the walls of Jericho, and *c*-a marching Israelite. How do you respond to what is happening? Why? 3/ How is this battle to be won? 4/ What is the meaning of Jericho being *devoted to the Lord for destruction?* 5/ Imagine the effect of deliverance on Rahab and her family. What happens to them? 6/ Compare verse 26 with 1 Kings 16:34. 7/ What do you learn here about God's word to and through men?

DAY *22* △ *Joshua 7*

1/ What does Joshua do in the face of failure? What are his concerns? 2/ How do you respond to unexpected and demoralizing failure? 3/ What is the reason for Israel's defeat? 4/ How does God view one man's sin (cf. v. 11)? What is God's remedy for the situation? Why is the penalty so severe (cf. 6:18-19; 7:11-12; Ex. 20:17)? 5/ How does Achan's sin affect his family and possessions?

6/ What does this chapter reveal about God's attitude toward sin? What is your attitude toward your sin?

DAY 23 △ Joshua 8

1/ What is the plan in this second attack on Ai? Where does Joshua get his strategy? 2/ What is the reason for Israel's victory? 3/ Why does Israel destroy all the people of Ai? 4/ Why does Joshua stop the campaign and build an altar? Compare the events of verses 30-35 with Deuteronomy 11:26-32 and 27:2-26. 5/ What is the place of the law of God in the life of this people? in your life?

DAY 24 △ Joshua 9

1/ Why do the Gibeonites devise their plan of deception? Why are the leaders of Israel fooled by them? 2/ What results among the people due to this failure? 3/ When you are a leader, what can you do to avoid this type of mistake? 4/ Why aren't the Gibeonites destroyed as the people of Jericho and Ai have been (cf. vv. 19-20, 24)? What does Joshua do to them? 5/ How do you feel about breaking your word (especially in a similarly deceptive situation)? 6/ Compare or contrast your position before God with the Gibeonites before Joshua. What do you learn from their attitude? 7/ Do you think the Gibeonites' sentence is a curse or a blessing? Why?

DAY 25 △ Joshua 10

1/ How is the Ammonites' reaction to the invading Israelites different from the Gibeonites'? Why, do you think, don't the Ammonites attack the Israelites directly? 2/ What does Joshua do when he hears of the attack on Gibeon? 3/ What is your responsibility to other Christians under attack? 4/ Describe the apparent physical condition of the Israelites (cf. v. 9 with 9:17). Where is their confidence placed? 5/ List all that the Lord does for Israel and Gibeon in this battle. Imagine the effect of the victory on the a-Gibeonites and b-Israelites. 6/ How does Joshua use this situation as a basis for engendering future trust in God? In what ways is God's presence and power in your life today related to your future situations? 7/ Why does Joshua completely destroy the Ammonite kings and people?

DAY 26 △ Joshua 11—12

1/ How is Israel's conquest of the north similar to its southern cam-

paign in chapter 10 (locate the lands on a map)?    2/ What underlies God's repeated command to his people, Do not be afraid (cf.
1:9; 8:1; 10:8; 11:6)? How can you be fearless in the face of the
aggression of nations today?    3/ Summarize the victories of Israel
so far.    4/ What is *a*-God's and *b*-the kings' part in coming to battle
with Israel? What is *a*-God's and *b*-the Israelites' part in overcoming
the lands (cf. previous chaps.; Deut. 9:4-5)? What does this indicate about God's relation to the movement of history?

### DAY 27   △   *Joshua 13*

1/ What does God point out to Joshua at the beginning of this
chapter?    2/ In what ways do you evaluate your present activities
in view of your goal in life? What do you discover?    3/ What does
God command Joshua to do now? How much of the land is not yet
conquered?    4/ Where is the land allotted to the two and a half
tribes?    5/ Why does God call this land an *inheritance* for Israel
(cf. Gen. 15:12-21; 17:7-8)? What has been the basis for their possession of it all along?    6/ What is the inheritance of Levi (cf.
Num. 18:19-24)?

### DAY 28   △   *Joshua 14–15*

1/ By what method is the land divided (cf. 14:2 with Num. 33:54)?
Who is making the decisions?    2/ What is the special request of
Caleb? Why does God give him the request (cf. Num. 14:24)?    3/
What about Caleb's character is revealed by his request? by his subsequent conquest?    4/ Of what tribe is Caleb a member? What
tribe's inheritance, by lot, is his land in?    5/ What do you learn
from these chapters about the promises and providence of God?

### DAY 29   △   *Joshua 16–19*

1/ Contrast the attitude of the tribe of Joseph with the attiude of
Caleb (cf. 14:12). How does Joshua answer Ephraim and Manasseh?
2/ What problem does Joshua point out in 18:3 (cf. 15:63; 16:10;
17:12-13; Num. 33:54-56)? What is the people's part to experience
full possession of their inheritance?    3/ What can you learn from
this principle?    4/ What principle underlies the Israelites' acceptance of inheritance by lot?    5/ Of what significance is God's sovereignty in your present situation? in your future?

DAY *30*   △   *Joshua 20–21*

1/ Analyze the pattern in 20:1-2, 7-8 and 21:2-3. What is God continually requiring from his people? What does this mean to you? 2/ What is the purpose of the cities of refuge (locate them on a map)? What does the command to establish them show about the nature of God?   3/ From where do the Levites receive their cities and pasture lands? How does this principle apply today?   4/ How many of the cities of refuge are inhabited by Levites? What, do you think, is the reason for this (cf. 18:7a)?   5/ What is the major thought of the writer in looking back over the partition of the land? 6/ In what *a*-past and *b*-recent situations have you experienced God's faithfulness?

## MONTH 10

DAY *1*   △   *Joshua 22*

1/ What is Joshua's primary concern for the Israelites who will be living on the other side of the Jordan? With what else is he concerned?   2/ What is the scope of your concern for other Christians? 3/ Why do the eastern tribes build an altar by the Jordan?   4/ To what motive do the other tribes attribute their action? What do the other tribes misunderstand?   5/ What can you learn from this event about your consideration for the actions of others? about your attitude toward those who have misunderstood your actions?   6/ Describe and imagine the religious life of Israel.

DAY *2*   △   *Joshua 23*

1/ What is Joshua's first reminder to the leaders of Israel? What fact about God does he again point out to them?   2/ What is God's promise to them? What are the conditions of the promise? Relate these conditions to the previous commands about their method of conquest (cf. 3:5; 6:17-18; chap. 7; 11:12-15).   3/ What attribute of God does Joshua praise in verse 14? How does this attitude of God relate to his promise of judgment?   4/ When you are a leader, what can you do to help insure purity of character in those for whom you are responsible?

DAY *3*   △   *Joshua 24*

1/ What does Joshua emphasize in his review of Israel's history in the presence of all the people (cf. Ex. 3:23-33)?   2/ What is the acceptable response he urges on Israel? Underline the verb (used sixteen times). What does this thought indicate about a-the Israelites and b-your relationship with God?    3/ Why does Joshua refuse to accept the quick response of the people?    4/ What attributes of God does he stress? Summarize the qualities of God and their expression in this book.    5/ How are you affected by these aspects of God's nature?    6/ What does Joshua tell the people about making a covenant with God (cf. 23:15-16)?    7/ Summarize a-the quality of Joshua's leadership and b-the response of the people in this book.

DAY 4    △    *Introduction to Galatians*

These Gentile Christians (possibly in Derbe, Lystra, Iconium, and Pisidian Antioch in Southern Galatia) have been converted from heathenism during Paul's first missionary journey. Some Jewish Christians are trying to impose the Jewish ritual and moral law on them. Paul is now compelled to write them this vigorous letter (probably A.D. 48-49).    1/ Read through the book at one sitting.    2/ What is Paul's tone in writing?    3/ List briefly the contrasts found throughout the letter between the *gospel of Christ* and the *perverted gospel.*    4/ Which of these qualities in the lists characterize your life?    5/ What is the origin of the gospel Paul preaches?

DAY 5    △    *Galatians 1:1-10*

1/ How does Paul introduce himself? Who is the source of his authority?    2/ What is the relationship of *grace* and *peace* to the things Christ has done for them and you?    3/ To what extent does Paul have confidence in the gospel he preaches?    4/ How can you have a similar certainty in what you believe?    5/ Distinguish what would please a-God and b-men in this controversy.    6/ Whom do you want to please today?

DAY 6    △    *Galatians 1:11-24*

1/ How has Paul received the gospel (cf. Acts 9:1-19)?    2/ Characterize Paul's life before and after his conversion.    3/ How do the facts of his life substantiate the source of the gospel he now preaches?    4/ For what purpose has God saved Paul?    5/What is God's purpose in saving you and placing you in your present circumstances?    6/ Whom do you know that can be characterized

by the statement of verse 24?    7/ How can other people *glorify* God because of you?

### DAY 7    △    *Galatians 2:1-10*

1/ How does Paul's account of his contact with the Jerusalem leaders strengthen the case for his independent apostleship? On what grounds do they accept him (cf. 1:1)?    2/ What is the content of the gospel to the circumcised? of the gospel to the uncircumcised? 3/ How would adding circumcision to the gospel make Paul *run in vain* and bring the Gentile Christians into bondage?    4/ Does the gospel you give to others lead them into freedom or bondage? 5/ What additional sphere of service does Peter request Paul to remember?    6/ How can you be concerned with the poor around you?

### DAY 8    △    *Galatians 2:11—3:1*

1/ What different ways of thinking do Peter (Cephas) and Paul represent?    2/ What makes Peter change his mind about eating with Gentile Christians (cf. Acts 10:28, 11:1-18)?    3/ How do Peter's actions affect the others?    4/ Why do Paul oppose Peter's change in thinking?    5/ List the two ways of being justified (although Paul condemns the one even as he states it).    6/ In each case on whose action does justification depend?    7/ Which way actually nullifies God's grace and makes Christ's death of no purpose?    8/ Why can't this way ever again be possible to Paul in view of verse 20?    9/ How does this fact explain Paul's action toward Peter and his vigorous judgment of those who present a "different" gospel (cf. 1:6-9)?    10/ Which gospel does your life portray?

### DAY 9    △    *Galatians 3:2-9*

1/ On what basis does a person *receive the Spirit?*    2/ When does this happen? Who gives the Spirit?    3/ How does these additions to the gospel contradict the way the Galatians have received the Spirit?    4/ How have you recently tried to perfect your life in Christ (which has begun supernaturally) by some natural means? How is this action foolish?    5/ How had Abraham become righteous? Did he have the law of Moses?    6/ In what way are you a son of Abraham? How is this fact important?    7/ What had Abraham

95

believed (cf. Gen. 15:1-6)?   8/ What specific promise or commandment is God asking you to believe (act on) today?

DAY 10  △  *Galatians 3:10-14*

1/ Contrast *men of faith* with *all who rely on works of the law.*
Which do *a*-the "circumcision party" and *b*-you belong to?   2/
Have you ever broken one of God's laws? What is God's right judgment on you?   3/ Can you erase past guilt by trying harder to
obey the law in the present? Whom do you know trying to do this?
What is the result?   4/ Does the law justly punish two men for a
single act of lawlessness? Who is the guilty party?   5/ Who has
brought you out of the curse (punishment) of the law? How? Why?
6/ According to Paul what is the fulfillment of God's promise to
Abraham?

DAY 11  △  *Galatians 3:15-18*

1/ Is any condition laid on Abraham to receive the promise (cf.
Gen. 15:1-21)? Are any conditions laid on the people (cf. Ex. 19:
3-9)?   2/ Compare and contrast these two events.   3/ How does
Paul refute the objection that the law of Moses annuls the promise
to Abraham and show the priority of faith?   4/ How do you receive the *inheritance* of salvation?

DAY 12  △  *Galatians 3:19-29*

1/ Underline the references to *a-promise, b-law* (scripture), and
*c-faith.*   2/ List what the *law a*-does and *b*-cannot do.   3/ How
does Paul answer, *Why then the law?*   4/ Since the *law* does not
invalidate *promise,* why is the *law* not antagonistic to *promise?*   5/
List what *faith* does. Compare what *faith* does with what the *law*
cannot do.   6/ To whom are all the *promises* of God to Abraham
given (v. 16)?   7/How then are these *promises* rightly made avail-
able to others, including yourself (v. 27)? (For the meaning of
*baptism* as used here cf. Rom. 6:3-11.)   8/ Since the only possible
way to become a *son* is through identification with Christ by *faith,*
is any social, political, racial, etc. difference among believers able
to divide their unity?   9/ How can you display this oneness with
other believers in Christ today?

DAY 13  △  *Galatians 4:1-11*

1/ How does Paul illustrate the condition of men before Christ?

Are men still so enslaved today?   2/ List the blessings and privileges which are yours through God's Son being born in this world. 3/ Contrast the former condition of the Galatians with the spiritual wealth they now have in Christ.   4/ In what ways do they act as in their former predicament?   5/ Have you been approached by groups which claim to lead you into new "truth" and new "ways" to gain Christ's benefits? How can you be true to the gospel in the face of this kind of error?

### DAY 14   △   *Galatians 4:12-20*

1/ What does this section reveal about the motivation of others who have developed an interest in the Galatians?   2/ What motivates Paul?   3/ Contrast the former and present relations of Paul and the Galatians. What makes the difference?   4/ How does this explain the intensity of Paul's argument in this letter?   5/ What are the tests which Paul uses to check a relationship to determine if it is sound?   6/ Who is concerned about you? How do you respond to them?   7/ Whom are you similarly concerned about? How can you express this concern for them today?

### DAY 15   △   *Galatians 4:21–5:1*

1/ How does Paul argue from his opponents' own terms?   2/ Contrast Abraham's two sons and what they represent (cf. Gen. 16:1-3, 15; 17:15-21; 21:1-2, 8-12).   3/ Whom are you like? Why?   4/ To whom does Paul liken the propagators of a different gospel? Why?   5/ List in two columns the contrasting ideas in the allegory. 6/ In what ways does the scripture cited in verse 30 make possible Paul's attitude toward the *false brethren* (cf. 1:7-9)?   7/ What are the responsibilities of being made free in Christ? How will you exercise them today?

### DAY 16   △   *Galatians 5:2-12*

1/ What is significant about Paul's reemphasis of who is speaking (cf. 1:1, 11-24)?   2/ Where is the authoritative gospel of the apostles found today? Are you constantly checking the gospel you live by and present to others against this authoritative source?   3/ What are the consequences if someone who has professed justification by faith in Christ now begins to also trust in his own activity to give him acceptance with God?   4/ What contemporary beliefs attempt to add other things to the gospel (cf. 4:8-10) Which do you find in your life? 5/ Being justified, what is your hope as a believer? How does this fact affect your attitude toward *a*-yourself, *b*-others (esp. non-Christians) and *c*-God? 6/ Contrast the bondage of outward observance with the freedom in Christ Jesus.

### DAY *17*  △  *Galatians 5:13-24*

1/ What is the freedom to which you have been *called* (cf. 5:1)? 2/ What are the practical limits and responsibilities of this freedom? 3/ Characterize the antithetical ways of living (*flesh* here means the whole personality of man organized for its own ends). 4/ Determine the meaning of each word in both lists. Distinguish which are *a*-Godward, *b*-manward, and *c*-selfward. 5/ How does each list relate to the law? 6/ In what specific areas of your life are you keenly aware of the desires of the flesh? How does your identification with Christ (cf. 2:20; 3:27) relate to these problems? 7/ Distinguish a realistic expectation of human nature from pessimism. 8/ In what particular situation today will you *serve* someone *through love?* How? 9/ How can you *walk* by the Spirit today? in the future?

### DAY *18*  △  *Galatians 5:25—6:10*

1/ What are the attitudes you must develop toward *a*-yourself and *b*-others if you are to walk by the Spirit (cf. 5:14)? 2/ What is the *law of Christ?* 3/ Explain from their context why verses 2 and 5 are not contradictory. 4/ How can you share *good things* with those who teach you the Bible? 5/ What is the cause and effect relationship of life for man (vv. 7-9)? 6/ Contrast *corruption* with *eternal life* (note the increased yield in both cases). 7/ What will hinder the reaping? 8/ In today's schedule how will you *do good* to some specific individuals?

### DAY *19*  △  *Galatians 6:11-18*

1/ What are the motives of the false teachers? How are they inconsistent? What do these motives reveal about them? 2/ What motivates Paul? 3/ Instead of circumcision what *marks* does Paul bear? 4/ How has Paul become a new creation (cf. 2:20)? Have you made Paul's statement your own? 5/ Summarize briefly *a*-the important issue at stake here, *b*-the two alternatives, and *c*-Paul's assertions about the issue. 6/ Summarize the marks of a false gospel (cf. 2:21; 3:12; 4:3, 10; 5:4) and the marks of the gospel of Christ (cf. 1:11-12; 2:20; 3:14, 22, 27-28; 4:6; 5:24). What does the law accomplish in each gospel? How is a person made righteous in each case? 7/ Imagine you are a Galatian in this situation. How do Paul's personal, historical, exegetical, and moral arguments convince you of your error? 8/ How is the gospel of Christ changing your daily life?

### DAY 20    △    *Exodus 21*

1/What is the situation in which these laws are given? How have the Israelites gotten here? 2/ Contrast the master—slave relationships here with what you know of the Israelites' position in Egypt. On what basis is the slavery permanent? 3/ List the crimes and misdemeanors in verses 12-35. Which of the commandments in chapter 20 are elaborated here? Which call for capital punishment? for punishment of another nature? Account for the distinction. 4/ Compare verses 15 and 17 with 20:12. Evaluate your attitude toward your parents in view of this standard. Imagine you are an Israelite. Do you expect long life or stand under the death penalty? How can you show *honor* to your parents today? 5/ What is to be the attitude toward the person and possessions of others? 6/ What belonging of someone should you replace because of your misuse or carelessness (cf. vv. 33-34)? 7/ How does knowing God make a difference in your relationships with others? 8/ By what scale of justice do you measure your life?

### DAY 21    △    *Exodus 22:1-15*

1/ What penalty is laid out for deliberate theft? 2/ How suitable is this sliding scale? 3/ List the careless acts which are under the law and the penalty for each. How does the penalty differ from that for deliberate theft? 4/ In which is the borrower not held responsible? On what basis? 5/ How can a person prove his innocence? 6/ Is your conduct and attitude toward God such that your word, before God, can establish your innocence? 7/ In this elaboration of the eighth commandment what about the justice of God is reflected in his instruction for the attitude toward that which belongs to others? 8/ Do you have a concern for others that extends to their possessions? In what ways do you fall short of this standard?

### DAY 22    △    *Exodus 22:16-31*

1/ Explain the relationship between sexual perversion and spiritual perversion. 2/ In view of pagan fertility rites and sacrifices relate verse 20 specifically to the acts of perversion described in verses 16-19.   3/ How does the attitude toward those in need illustrate the mercy and compassion of God?   4/ What characteristics of God does the penalty for disobedience to these principles illustrate? 5/ Is it possible to love and serve God and be indifferent to the physical needs of others? What can you do about this today?   6/ Measure your attitude toward specific authority against the command in verse 28.   7/ To what areas does the principle developed in verses 29-31 extend for the Israelites?   8/ What object lesson does God use to remind Israel that he is to be absolutely first?   9/ List the things you give to God. How do they relate to your priorities? How are you going to give him first place in the future?   10/ Summarize the quality of life to characterize God's people. How can this quality become a reality in your life?

### DAY 23   △   *Exodus 23:1-19*

1/ Summarize the content of each of the specific commands in verses 1-8.   2/ What quality of life is God seeking to develop in his people here? What does this reflect of his own nature?   3/ What characteristics of his nature is God seeking to be evident in his people in verse 9 (cf. 22:21-27)?   4/ What needs do the commands of verses 10-13 meet?   5/ What changes can you make so that a day of rest is a time of renewal instead of frantic activity for you and others?   6/ Recall the original command given to Israel concerning the passover and the purpose of the memorial feast. What other two occasions are they to celebrate?   7/ When and how do you express gratitude to God?   8/ How does verse 19$^b$ relate to harvesting (this is a Canaanite magical technique to produce early rains)?   9/ What do you give God in expenditure of the honest results of your work (cf. his command to Israel here)?

### DAY 24   △   *Exodus 23:20-33*

1/ What are the provisional conditions and promises God makes? 2/ What is the reason for the seriousness of God's demand for obedience?   3/ Account for the necessity of driving the pagan tribes out of the land. Why doesn't God get rid of all of them at once and thus eliminate temptation?   4/ What compromises that you have made are now a *snare* to you in your full obedience and worship to the Lord? How can you disengage yourself from any of those which are temporary or non-covenant? 5/ Summarize the areas in which God will bless Israel if they serve him. 6/ Do you have any real needs God has not fully met? Relate these to the extent of your commitment and obedience to him. Have you failed to meet God's standard or has he reneged on his word?

DAY 25  △  *Exodus 24*

1/ How do the people respond when Moses relays God's message to them? 2/ How and where is this agreement ratified? 3/ Describe God as seen by the seventy-four leaders. What kind of men are the leaders (cf. 18:21)? 4/ What is the significance of verse 11 (cf. 19:12-13, 21-22)? 5/ What privilege does God allow Moses? 6/ How does God's glory appear to the people below? 7/ Contrast the three groups of people mentioned in this chapter as to a-number, b-privilege given, c-intimacy with God, and d-view of God from each perspective. Account, if possible, for the difference between each grouping. 8/ What is your goal as to knowing God? Compare or contrast your goal with what the three groups in this chapter know of God. 9/ What areas of your life need to be brought into obedience to God today to have deepened knowledge of God?

DAY 26  △  *Exodus 25:1-22*

1/ What command does God give Moses? Who is to participate? 2/ What are the gifts' a-variety and b-value (cf. 11:2-3; 12:35-36)? 3/ What is the use of these gifts now? 4/ What is the purpose of the sanctuary? Who is to draw up the blueprint? 5/ Draw a mental picture of each sanctuary item (continue in subsequent chapters). Imagine the materials and workmanship. 6/ What is to be put in the *ark*? What is on top? 7/ What is the purpose and significance of the ark? 8/ Recount how God has taken the initiative in meeting and speaking with you. Do you seek opportunities to meet him and to listen to his orders?

DAY 27  △  *Exodus 25:23-40*

1/ Imagine the craftsmanship and delicate detail work in each piece. 2/ What skills can you use in worship and service to the Lord? 3/ Determine the significance of a-incense, b-libation, and c-bread of the Presence in connection with the *table*. 4/ What is the source of your nourishment? 5/ What means does God ordain to illuminate the interior?   6/ What command does God repeat (cf. v. 9)?   7/ To what extent does God govern the specific details of your life?

### DAY 28   △   *Exodus 26*

1/ Imagine the workmanship of the *linen curtains*. What are the dimensions? the unifying factors?   2/ What is the relationship of the linen curtains, the goats' hair curtains, and the leather tent?   3/ Contrast the appearance of the tabernacle from the outside (with natural light) to the inside.   4/ What is the balance between beauty and function? Which is most obvious?   5/ How much time do you give to cultivating internal beauty in proportion to external attractiveness?   6/ In observing the physical world what is the balance between beauty and function? In what ways do you reveal an appreciation for God's encompassing protection and the expression of himself in beauty?   7/ Where is the *veil* to be hung? What is its purpose?   8/ Where is the ark located in relation to the veil? to the other furnishings mentioned so far?

### DAY 29   △   *Exodus 27*

1/ What is the function of the *altar*?   2/ How often is the command *as it has been shown you on the mountain* repeated in the instructions for the tabernacle?   3/ Compare or contrast this emphasis on obedience to your attitude toward obedience.   4/ Compare the construction of the outer court in size and materials with that of the inner (or holy) places.   5/ What insurance is made for the lamp? Account for the need of continual lighting in the context of the tabernacle construction.   6/ What about the character of God is reflected in the construction and furnishing of the tabernacle?

### DAY 30   △   *Exodus 28*

1/ Who are to serve God as priests? Why are they to be dressed differently?   2/ Who is to make this clothing? What is the source of their ability?   3/ Contrast this recorded fact with contemporary opinion about wisdom and ability.   4/ List and describe each garment as to *a*-particular features, *b*-specific reasons or purposes, and *c*-where the garment or special features are worn. From this determine the responsibility given to Aaron.   5/ What is the relation of art and religion?   6/ What are the prerequisites of service as a priest?   7/ What are the consequences of failure to comply to the details of the instructions?   8/ Is God more lenient in asking for your obedience and allegiance? Are your motives for obeying based on his command or on your feelings at the moment?

## MONTH 11

### DAY 1   △   Exodus 29:1-37

1/ List each step in the consecration of verses 1-9.   2/ Distinguish the offerings to be made. What is the significance of their order? 3/ Project and imagine the feelings of Aaron and his sons concerning their clothing, the ceremony, and the instructions about the offerings.   4/ Compare the different ways in which Aaron and his sons identify with each offering. Determine the significance of each means of identification in view of the offering.   5/ How have you identified with Christ as your sin offering?   6/ What three parts of Aaron's and his sons' bodies are consecrated with the blood of the second ram? In what order? Why, do you think?   7/ What is to happen to the flesh of the ram of ordination?   8/ How long is the ceremony of atonement and consecration to last?   9/ What special "precaution" is taken with regard to the altar?

### DAY 2   △   Exodus 29:38—30:38

1/ Describe the *burnt offering* as to *a*-nature of offering, *b*-frequency, and *c*-termination.   2/ What is the purpose of the *tent of meeting*? How is it sanctified?   3/ What is God's promise to Israel and their anticipated response?   4/ On what basis do you know the Lord is your God? In what way does he *dwell* with you?   5/ How often is the *altar of incense* used? When is atonement for it to be made? How?   6/ Describe the census tax. For what is it to be used?   7/ What is the function of the *laver*? What is its significance? What is the penalty for disregarding its function?   8/ Contrast the uses of the *anointing oil* and the *incense*. Determine the significance of each.   9/ What is the penalty for counterfeiting? 10/ How do these objects, functions, and penalties reflect the character of God (cf. v. 10)?

### DAY 3   △   Exodus 31

1/ Summarize verse 1-11 as to *a*-whom God chooses to do his work, *b*-what "equipment" he gives them, and *c*-what they are to do.   2/ What is the Spirit of God's relation to *artistic design*? What effect

103

does this have on your evaluation of yourself? of others?   3/   What is your attitude toward physical work? toward those whom God has equipped to work with material things?   4/ What added significance is given to the sabbath (cf. 20:8-11)?   5/ Identify the characteristics in your life which a-reflect God's creative activity and b-uniquely distinguish you as one set apart by the Lord.   6/ What are the two significant factors about the stone tablets?   7/ Imagine you are in Moses' sandals. How highly do you value these tablets for what they represent?   8/ How highly do you view the Bible as the word of God?

DAY 4   △   *Exodus 32:1-14*

1/ How long is Moses away?   2/ Whom do the people look to for leadership?   3/ Contrast their request with God's commands and their commitment six weeks before (cf. 20:3-4; 19:8).   4/ What specific commitments have to be made to God? How long do you remember and practice these solemn promises?   5/ Contrast Aaron's privileged experience six weeks before (24:9-11) with his actions now. How does he try to appease the people?   6/ How do the people respond to his creation? In what further ways does Aaron encourage their sin? What is the significance of verse 5?   7/ How do you respond when God's actions seem delayed?   8/ What are the implications of taking matters into your own hands in your role as a leader or example to others?   9/ What is the Lord's analysis and judgment of this situation?   10/ List the reasons Moses uses in interceding for Israel. What is the basis for his plea?   11/ Analyze Moses' attitude in view of verse 10b. What effect does he have?   12/ Determine the meaning of *repent* and *evil* as used in verse 14. Reconcile this with what you have learned of God's holiness and righteousness. What is the essential meaning of verse 14?

DAY 5   △   *Exodus 32:15-35*

1/ Reconstruct the events when Moses comes down the mountain. 2/ Contrast the attitudes and actions of Moses, Aaron, and the Levites. How does Moses' attitude differ from when the Lord first tells him about the idolatry?   3/ Whom does Moses hold accountable?   4/ What is Aaron's reply? In what ways does his answer differ from the record in verses 1-6?   5/ When called for an account, do you give all the facts (even when they expose your sin)?

6/ What qualities of leadership do you observe in Moses?  7/ In what ways do the Levites prove themselves fit for the service of the Lord?  8/ Having dealt in judgment with the sin, what is Moses' next step? Describe his attitude.  9/ What is God's answer for the people? for Moses? for the future?  10/ What is your attitude toward your sin and its consequences?  11/ Can you intercede with fervency after administering discipline?  12/ Compare the qualities of justice and mercy shown by Moses to illustrate characteristics of God.

### DAY 6  △  *Exodus 33*

1/ List the promises in this chapter to a-Israel and b-Moses. What is the basis or reason for each?  2/ What culminating event finally results in Israel's repentance?  3/ What indicates that they will not soon forget this (vv. 5-6)? Contrast this to the use of ornaments in chapter 32.  4/ What is Moses' regular habit? Who goes with him?  5/ What evidences that he actually meets God there? What kind of relationship exists?  6/ Analyze Moses' conversation with God as to a-his requests, b-the basis for the requests, and c-God's response.  7/ What evidences that Israel is different from other nations and tribes? How is this related to God's sovereignty?  8/ What instructions does the Lord give in answer to Moses' last bold request? Why can't Moses see God's *face?*  9/ Characterize your relationship with God. Are you more concerned with knowing him or receiving from him? What are the effects of your attitude in your life?  10/What steps will you take today toward an intimate friendship?

### DAY 7  △  *Exodus 34*

1/ What further preparations is Moses to make for this summit conference?  2/ To determine the meaning of *the Lord . . . proclaimed the name of the Lord* (v. 5) enumerate the characteristics which he describes.  3/ Distinguish the meaning of each.  4/ What is Moses' immediate reaction? Contrast his prayer of verse 9 with his previous demands (33:12-18). Account for his changed attitude.  5/ Compare verses 9-10 to determine Moses' request and the Lord's response. Which of the Lord's attributes (vv. 6-7) do these illustrate?  6/ What are the terms of the covenant (vv. 10-11)?  7/ Though God forgives sin, does this imply lowered or altered standards?  8/ List the essence of each command in verses 11-26.  9/ What priority is to be given to God in worship? in work? in rest?  10/ What is the effect of this summit conference as far as a-God, b-Moses, and c-the people are concerned?   11/ In what ways do people around you know you have been with God?   12/ List the specific differences you have experienced in your life because of knowing God intimately.

DAY 8   △   *Exodus 35*

1/ Compare this emphasis on the sabbath with 20:8; 23:12; 31:12-17; and 34:21. What are the reasons given? Describe the relationship to the context for each.   2/ In view of this command in the context of the building of the tabernacle (even work dedicated to the Lord is stopped—lighting fires) what emphasis, do you think, should you place on a day of rest?   3/ List the items for which Moses requests materials. Does he omit anything concerning the Lord's command (cf. 25:2-7)?   4/ In verses 20-29 list the indications of motivation for giving.   5/ What motivates you to give: legalism? rivalry with others? pressure? tax advantages? needs of others? the Spirit of the Lord?   6/ What do you give?   7/ What is the important difference in verses 30-35 from 31:1-11?   8/ How does this affect the scope of your work? all work?

DAY 9   △   *Exodus 36:1–39:31*

1/ What command does Moses give? Why?   2/ Begin a sketch of the tabernacle as it is built. List the order of construction.   3/ What is the significance of the purposes of the furniture and priestly garb to the tabernacle?   4/ Imagine the weight and size of the completed structure. What features are built into it for mobility (e.g. 36:8-9, 20-22; 37:1-5)? for solidarity (cf. 38:27-31)?   5/ Underline every evidence of obedience to the blueprint and patterns.   6/ How does this reflect Moses' ability to communicate?   7/ Do you give God haphazard service or full obedience in details?

DAY 10   △   *Exodus 39:42–40:38*

1/ Underline all references to obedience.   2/ What evidences that Moses approves of the finished construction (39:43)?   3/ What is the time lapse between the erection of the tabernacle and the beginning of worship in it (40:1, 17)?   4/ Distinguish the logical order of erecting and furnishing the tabernacle (cf. 40:1-8, 18-33).   5/ Is your life characterized by disorder and impatience or by orderliness and the ability to wait?   6/ Cite the evidence of God's approval.  7/ How is the center of worship related to further guidance? Compare 40:36-38 with 33:14 to determine the fulfillment of promise.  8/ Who do you look to for guidance?

### DAY 11  △  Exodus 1—40

1/ Trace Moses' development as a leader.  2/ What characteristics that you have observed in him will you incorporate in your life?  3/ What aspects of God's promises in 6:5-8 have been fulfilled? What are yet unfulfilled?  5/ Contrast the status of Israel prior to 19:1-6 with their identity and development as a nation thereafter. 6/ What is the place of the law? of worship? Account for the activity of God in this development from slaves to a holy nation.  7/ What are the main emphases of this book concerning the character of God?  8/ In what ways has your view of God been altered or enlarged? What effect does this have on your view of the kind of person you should and want to be?  9/ What principles or applications have you incorporated into your life? What additional steps of obedience do you need to take?

### DAY 12  △  Introduction to Romans

Paul writes this letter to the church at Rome (which he has never as yet visited) while in Corinth on his third missionary journey. He introduces himself and gives a detailed explanation of the gospel. His desire to visit the center of the empire is fulfilled three years later when he arrives as a prisoner (cf. Acts 28:16-31). Romans 1:1-7 1/ In what way does Paul introduce himself? What does this description reveal about his view of himself?  2/ Characterize the recipients of the letter. Imagine how they (as a despised minority) respond to the fact that they are called and beloved.  3/ How do you respond to these facts?  4/ Describe the gospel as to its a-origin, b-content, c-power, d-proclamation, and e-destination.  5/ How should these facts affect your attitude toward the Old Testament? toward missions?  6/ What periods in Christ's life does Paul emphasize? How does each show that Christ is the a-center of the gospel and b-stimulus for proclaiming it?

### DAY 13  △  Romans 1:8-15

1/ Describe Paul's attitude toward the Roman Christians.  2/ For what reasons does he want to visit them?  3/ What is the content of his prayers about them?  4/ What Christian can you pray for in

this way? 5/ What claims does Paul make? Why should this educated, cultured man consider himself *under obligation* to all men?
6/ Contrast or compare his attitude with your present attitude. What
types of people do you exclude from these categories?

### DAY 14 △ *Romans 1:16-17*

1/ List the facts about the gospel (cf. vv. 1-6, 15). 2/ What is
the significance of *for* in verses 16-17? 3/ Relate the first phrase
of verse 16 with the situation in Rome. 4/ Why is the gospel pow-
erful? How is its power released? 5/ How is *faith* related to *salvation* and the *righteousness of God?* 6/ What is different about living by *faith* rather than by *a*-sight, *b*-works, or *c*-feelings?

### DAY 15 △ *Romans 1:18-23*

1/ How are God's *righteousness* (v. 17) and his *wrath* (v. 18) related? 2/ What actions of man prompt God's wrath? 3/ Characterize man's sin from *a*-what he chooses not to do and *b*-what he
does instead. 4/ How do these actions affect man's intellectual and
spiritual life? In what ways are the actions *foolish?* 5/ Why is every
man (even those in primitive societies) *without excuse?* 6/ To
what extent are you honoring God as God and being thankful? 7/
What form does idolatry take for you today?

### DAY 16 △ *Romans 1:24-32*

1/ How is God's repeated action (vv. 24, 26, 28) related to the
expression of wrath in verse 18? 2/ How is being allowed to have
your own way a punishment? 3/ How does man react to being
*given up?* 4/ Group the sins in verses 29-31 under *a-base mind*
and *b-improper conduct.* In what ways does this list differ from what
today's society considers sins? 5/ Why, do you think, are no de-
grees of sin given? 6/ From what do all these sins stem (cf. vv.
21, 25, 28, 32)? 7/ How does Paul show that these sins are *a*-cal-
culated and *b*-propagated?

### DAY 17 △ *Romans 2:1-11*

1/ Of what does Paul accuse the Jews who have the revelation of
God's law? 2/ What is Paul trying to clarify by his three questions
in verses 3-4? 3/ What should be the response to God's kindness
and patience? 4/ Contrast the *riches* (v. 4) with what is *stored up*
(v. 5). 5/ Describe God's judgment. 6/ Upon what will men be

judged? What changes do you need to make in your life in view of the basis of judgment?

DAY *18* △ *Romans 2:12-16*

1/ On what basis will God judge the Jews who have the law? 2/ How will he judge the Gentiles who have no written law? Where is their *law?* 3/ Further describe God's judgment (cf. vv. 1-11). 4/ Contrast God's judgment with man's judgment (v. 1). 5/ What is your prayer today to this judge?

DAY *19* △ *Romans 2:17-29*

1/ For what reasons do the Jews compliment themselves? 2/ Of what does Paul accuse them? 3/ How have they *blasphemed* God's name? How have you? 4/ In what ways does the accusation of verses 17-24 fit you and your Christian group? 5/ What is required of the Jews if their outward religious symbol (circumcision) is to have meaning? 6/ What will give meaning to your outward religious performance? 7/ Whose praise do you seek?

DAY *20* △ *Romans 3:1-18*

1/ What objections to his condemnation of Jewish "righteousness" (in chap. 2) does Paul anticipate (vv. 1, 3, 5, 7-8)? 2/ How does Paul answer each objection briefly? 3/ What attributes of God remain unchanged? 4/ To what kind of people do you feel superior due to your specific advantages? 5/ By using Old Testament quotations how does Paul verify his contention about all men in verse 9? 6/ From the quotations characterize man as to his *a*-attitudes, *b*-direction, *c*-speech, and *d*-pursuits. 7/ Where do you fit into this characterization? 8/ Compare these quotations with the picture of man in 1:18-32.

DAY *21* △ *Romans 3:19-20*

1/ All of the above brings Paul to what conclusions about the purpose of the law? 2/ Who is included in those held accountable before God? 3/ Determine the meaning of *justification.* 4/ What way of justification is blocked in verse 20? 5/ What function does the law have? 6/ Why is it impossible for you to be justified before God by your own efforts?

109

DAY 22  △  *Romans 3:21-31*

1/ Since legal obedience cannot make man acceptable to God, what will? 2/ How has 1:18—3:18 prepared you to consider God's way of righteousness? 3/ List and explain what is involved in God's way of righteousness. 4/ Who takes the initiative in providing a way to be justified? 5/ On what conditions is a person justified? 6/ In view of God's way of righteousness what happens to your pride and boasting? Why?

DAY 23  △  *Romans 4:1-12*

1/ What possible reaction to chapter 3 does Paul anticipate from his Jewish readers? 2/ How does Abraham receive right standing with God (cf. Paul's arguments in Gal. 3:6-18; 4:21-31)? 3/ Why can't Abraham boast before God or *claim his due?* 4/ When is he reckoned righteous (cf. Gen. 15; 17)? By whom? On what basis? 5/ What is the significance of circumcision in his life? 6/ Who are the children of Abraham? 7/ How does this way of righteousness affect your attitude toward God? toward good works?

DAY 24  △  *Romans 4:13-25*

1/ To whom is the *promise* (cf. Gen. 12:1-3, 7) made? On what does it depend? Why? 2/ From verses 18-25 list the five ways Abraham reacts to God's promise (cf. Gen. 15; 17). 3/ What circumstances are "incredible"? 4/ In what ways and situations do you *believe* in spite of circumstances? 5/ What is the result of Abraham's faith in an "incredible" promise? 6/ Compare what *a*-Abraham (v. 17b) and *b*-you (v. 24) have to believe about God to be righteous. 7/ What is the purpose of Jesus' death and resurrection? 8/ What about Abraham's faith needs to be true of your faith?

DAY 25  △  *Romans 5:1-11*

1/ List the consequences of justification by faith (by Christ's blood, death, and life). Which concern God's legal requirements? your life on earth? 2/ In what three things are you to rejoice? What has caused you to rejoice recently? What have been the results? 3/ Trace the progression and results of suffering. 4/ Contrast the Christian's past (vv. 6, 8, 10) with his present and future (vv. 9-11). 5/ How is God's love related to each needed change? 6/ How is

the security of a Christian related to *much more* in verses 9-10?    7/
How can you worship God for his love to you today?

### DAY 26 △ *Romans 5:12-21*

1/ What do you learn here about sin and death? Which comes first?
With what effects?    2/ List the contrasts between Adam and Christ
as representatives of the human race.    3/ What is the *free gift?*
4/ What are the results of Adam's trespass and Christ's free gift?
5/ Summarize the effect of the law on sin (cf. vv. 13, 20 with 3:19-
20).    6/ How is God's grace *much more* than a match for sin?
7/ How can you move from the *reign of sin and death* to the *reign
of life?*

### DAY 27 △ *Romans 6:1-11*

1/ What is the theme of this section?    2/ What experiences have
all Christians shared with Christ? With what results?    3/ In what
ways do you exploit God's grace? Why?    4/ What does the Christian *know* in verses 9-11?    5/ What is he to do in view of this
knowledge?    6/ What difference does this fact make in your attitude and action toward sin and temptation in your life?

### DAY 28 △ *Romans 6:12-23*

1/ In order to live consistent with his position in Christ what must
a Christian do? not do?    2/ What role does your will have in de-
ciding what has dominion over you?    3/ In what ways will you
*yield your members* (physical and mental) today? How will this act
affect you? others?    4/ Contrast the two possible *masters* a person
can choose. What are the consequences of each slavery?    5/ How
does *yielding* relate to the fact of *belonging* (as in the master—slave
relationship)?    6/ Describe the past, present, and future of the
Christian.    7/ How is *sanctification* obtained (vv. 17, 19, 22-23)?
8/ How does verse 23 show that sanctification does not earn eternal
life?

### DAY 29 △ *Romans 7:1-6*

1/ What analogy does Paul use to show the Christian's relationship
to the law?    2/ How does a person get free from the demands of
the law?    3/ Summarize the point of the illustration in verses 2-3.
4/ What application does Paul make in verse 4?    5/ What new
relationship is established?    6/ Contrast the *fruit* of the past and

111

present.    7/ Compare or contrast the fruit you *bear* with 6:10, 13, 17, and 19.

DAY *30*  △  *Romans 7:7-13*

1/ How does Paul show that the law and sin are not identical? How are they related?    2/ What is the purpose of the law?    3/ What does the law reveal to *a*-Paul and *b*-you?    4/ How do you react to prohibitions?    5/ How is sin personified?    6/ What effects does sin produce in *a*-Paul's and *b*-your life?    7/ Paraphrase the conclusion about sin in verse 13.    8/ How does this passage show that you do not attain holy living by trying to keep rules?

## MONTH 12

DAY *1*  △  *Romans 7:14-25*

1/ What paradox does Paul experience (cf. Gal. 5:17)? Which force does he find stronger in his life?    2/ List what Paul *a*-can and *b*-cannot do. Relate verse 24 to this predicament.    3/ When do you experience this personal paradox? Why?    4/ Distinguish the two types of *law* here.    5/ What *a*-explanations and *b*-answer does Paul find to his struggle to please God by keeping the law of God?    6/ To what extent are you responsible for your actions?    7/ By what means are you trying to live pleasing to God? With what results?

DAY *2*  △  *Romans 8:1-11*

1/ How does Paul summarize his letter so far? On what relationship is this based?    2/ What reasons does Paul give in verses 2-4 for his confidence in verse 1?    3/ How can you be delivered from the struggle summarized in 7:14-25?    4/ List the contrasts between the two kinds of living in verses 4b-8.    5/ In verses 9-11 which of the two groups are addressed?    6/ What facts about them are true now? in the future?    7/ On what condition can these promises be yours?    8/ What do your actions reveal to people around you about your identification with one of the groups?

DAY *3*  △  *Romans 8:12-17*

1/ From verses 12-17 add to yesterday's list of facts about the two kind of living.    2/ Relate *put to death* (v. 13) to *set the mind* (vv. 4b-7) and *consider* and *yield* (6:11-13).    3/ Who empowers the Christian to live a holy life? to realize his relationship with God?

4/ Relate your relationship with God to the Roman custom of adoption (cf. Gal. 4:1-7).   5/ Contrast the two *spirits* in verse 15.   6/ List what each Christian has in common with Jesus Christ.   7/ To what extent are you enjoying these *a*-responsibilities and *b*-privileges of the Christian life?

DAY *4*   △   *Romans 8:18-25*

1/ How do these verses compliment 5:2-5?   2/ How are *suffering* and *glory* related (cf. v. 17)?   3/ What is the glory to be revealed? 4/ What conditions of *a*-creation and *b*-Christians are described here? What is each awaiting?   5/ How are the outcomes in verses 21 and 23 related?   6/ How is the presence of the Holy Spirit in your life related to the coming glory?   7/ In what ways is *hope* as much a part of the Christian life as faith?   8/ For what reasons do you have hope regardless of circumstances?

DAY *5*   △   *Romans 8:26-30*

1/ What else does the Spirit do for Christians (cf. v. 23)?   2/ What are the characteristics of the Spirit's prayers?   3/ How can they strengthen your prayer life?   4/ What additional assurance can you have in the face of suffering? What is *a*-God's and *b*-your part in that assurance?   5/ To what extent is God's goodness at work in the lives and circumstances of his people?   6/ Trace the progression of God's dealing with every Christian.   7/ What is his purpose in calling you? Relate this purpose to 5:2 and 8:18.   8/ How are you responding to God's high purposes for you?

DAY *6*   △   *Romans 8:31-39*

1/ How does this section give perspective to Paul's previous development of God's grace and man's suffering?   2/ What are specific evidences of God's love?   3/ What does verse 34 reveal about the person and work of Jesus Christ?   4/ Over what kinds of situations can the Christian be victorious? How may he *conquer?*   5/ How does the list of powers in verses 38-39 begin similar to but far exceed the list in verses 35-36?   6/ List the problems and obstacles that cause you to despair and suffer. What is the basis of your confidence for victory over these and circumstances of any kind? How dependable are your resources?

113

DAY 7  △  *Romans 1–8*

1/ Summarize the ways man is estranged from God.  2/ Summarize the reasons a-pagans (1:18-32), b-moralists (2:1-16), c-Jews (2:17–3:8), and d-you are inexcusable in rejecting God.  3/ Summarize how a-Old Testament patriarchs, b-Jews, c-Gentiles, and d-you can have right standing with God.  4/ List the before and after characteristics in your life.  5/ In what ways are you free from a-sin, b-the law, and c-death? How do these facts affect your daily living?

DAY 8  △  *Romans 9:1-5*

1/ In what ways does Paul establish his veracity? How does this relate to a possible misunderstanding as to Paul's attitude toward Jews (cf. previous chaps.)?  2/ What is the extent of Paul's concern for the Jews (cf. the meaning of *accursed* in Gal. 1:8-9; Josh. 6:17)?  3/ What concern do you have for the truthfulness of what you say? for those around you who have a mistaken idea about their relationship with God?  4/ What heritage belongs to the Jews (cf. Ex. 4:22, 19:16–21:1; 40:34-38)?  5/ How is Christ related to the Jews? supracultural?

DAY 9  △  *Romans 9:6-13*

1/ Why is the faithfulness of God's word not affected by Israel's unbelief?  2/ Who are the true descendants of Abraham (cf. 4:18-24; Gal. 3:29)?  3/ Who are the children of God? How do they become God's children?  4/ To whom are the promises given (cf. 4:12-13)?  5/ What principle is illustrated by Jacob and Esau?  6/ What is God's attitude toward you? What is your response to him?  7/ In what ways is God's *hate* different from man's hate?

DAY 10  △  *Romans 9:14-24*

1/ What objections does Paul anticipate to his statements in a-verses 6-13 and b-verse 18?  2/ How does he answer them?  3/ Does God exist for man's purposes or vice versa? How does this relate to ultimate authority and God's will?  4/ How is God's *mercy* based on his sovereignty?  5/ What are God's sovereign rights over men as sinners? To what purpose does God use them and their acts?  6/ How does Paul illustrate God's rights over all men?  7/ What is the significance to you to know you can't "make" God be merciful to you?  8/ In what ways do you respond to God's a-mercy and b-authority?

DAY *11*  △  *Romans 9:25-33*

1/ In what way does Paul apply Hosea's words to the Gentiles (cf. Hos. 1:2-11; 2:23)? How do they relate to the attributes of God as revealed in verses 6-24?  2/ How does Paul apply Isaiah's words to the previous statements about Israel (esp. v. 6)?  3/ What is the relation of human responsibility to the sovereignty of God?  4/ What is the ironical situation concerning Jews and Gentiles? Why? 5/ What are two responses to the *rock?* With which do you identify now? With what results?

DAY *12*  △  *Romans 10:1-10*

1/ Recall Paul's attitude for his *brethren* in chapter 9 (vv. 1-3). What is his action here?  2/ Determine what will *enlighten* the Jews' zeal.  3/ What people that you know have a similar ignorance of the way to attain righteousness? What can you do about it?  4/ Contrast the judgment of ignorance here with the contemporary popular opinion concerning responsibility when ignorant.  5/ Distinguish the two types of *righteousness* here.  6/ Where is true righteousness found? Contrast this with the extremes of verses 6-7. 7/ In what way do these questions (vv. 6-7) reflect unbelief?  8/ What must a person do to be *saved?*  9/ In what ways does the *a*-confession and *b*-belief relate to the unbelief in verses 6-7?  10/ How are confession and belief related in your life?

DAY *13*  △  *Romans 10:11-17*

1/ What is the reason God justifies Jews and Gentiles in the same way (cf. 3:29-30)?  2/ How does Paul confirm this principle from the Old Testament (cf. Gen. 12:8; 21:33; 26:25)?  3/ What is involved in to *call upon the name of the Lord?* Can belief exist in a vacuum?  4/ What is the content of what must be preached? Is this the content of your message? Why?  5/ What is your attitude toward those who do not *heed* the gospel (cf. Paul's concern in v. 1; 9:1-3)?

DAY *14*  △  *Romans 10:18-21*

1/ How does Paul show that hearing does not produce faith?  2/ How are faith and hearing related in your life (cf. v. 17)?  3/ To what extent is the gospel *heard* (cf. 1:19-20; Ps. 19)?  4/ What happens to Israel because of the extent of the gospel (v. 19)? To what extent does Israel *know* this is going to happen?  5/ Contrast

115

God's attitude toward the a-Gentiles (cf. 9:30) and b-Jews with Israel's attitude toward God (cf. 10:2).    6/ What is your attitude toward God? Why?    7/ What qualities of God are revealed by Isaiah's quotes?    8/ Summarize Paul's method in showing that Israel is inexcusable.

DAY 15    △    *Romans 11:1-6*

1/ What is a mistaken conclusion to the theme of chapter 10?    2/ In what ways does a-Paul's identity as a Jew, b-God's *foreknowledge* (cf. 9:6-13), and c-Elijah's experience (cf. 1 Kings 19:10, 14, 17-18) show that this conclusion is mistaken?    3/ What is God's action on the part of the *remnant* (cf. 9:27) of seven thousand men?    4/ Characterize God's *grace.* How is it antithetical to works (cf. 9:11)?    5/ What is your response to this God of grace?

DAY 16    △    *Romans 11:7-16*

1/ All of the above brings Paul to what summary?    2/ To which group do you belong? How do you know?    3/ How do the Old Testament quotations support verse 7?    4/ What are the normal and right functions and intent of *eyes, ears,* and *feasts* (cf. Ps. 69: 22-23)?    5/ How are these functions and intents reversed? For whom?    6/ Compare this characterization of Israel with the attitudes and activities of the Jews Paul encounters during his travels in *Acts.*    7/ What are God's purposes through the stumbling (v. 11) and rejection (v. 15) of Israel?    8/ How does the Jews' *full inclusion* relate to their *trespass* and *failure?*    9/ Why does Paul want to make the Jews *jealous?*    10/ Who are the *first fruits* and *root* (cf. v. 28)? What is their effect on Israel?    11/ Is God's rejection of Israel total? final?    12/ What qualities of God are revealed here?

DAY 17    △    *Romans 11:17-24*

1/ How does Paul illustrate his statements about Israel?    2/ Who are the *root* and *natural branches?* What has happened to some of the branches? Why?    3/ Who are the *wild shoots?* What is done to them? Why?    4/ What is the correct attitude of those identified by the wild shoots? Why?    5/ In what ways can the original process in Paul's analogy be reversed?    6/ How are God's *kindness, severity,* and *power* related?    7/ What is your attitude toward your part in God's plan? Why?

DAY *18*  △  *Romans 11:25-36*

1/ What is God's *mystery* concerning Jews and Gentiles?  2/ Determine the meaning of *all* in verse 26 (cf. vv. 12, 15, 23-24).  3/ What is the status of the Gentiles before God's mercy?  4/ What is the status of the Jews as Paul writes? in the future?  5/ How does Paul use Isaiah's (59:20-21) and Jeremiah's (31:33-34) words to support the truth of the future status of Israel?  6/ What is your attitude toward Old Testament scripture (cf. Paul's attitude here and in previous chaps.)?  7/ How can the Jews be both *enemies* and *beloved* at the same time?  8/ What is the relation of the disobedience of Israel to God's mercy to the Gentiles? of the disobedience of the Gentiles to God's mercy to the Jews?  9/ What is the only context in which *mercy* can have meaning?  10/ In what ways are verses 33-36 a fitting summary of the facts about Jews and Gentiles in chapters 9-11?  11/ In what ways will you share your knowledge of God's *mystery* with others today? in the future?

DAY *19*  △  *Romans 12:1-8*

1/ How does Paul's appeal relate to the new status you have in Christ (cf. 6:1–7:6)?  2/ What commands relate to the body? to the mind? What is the standard?  3/ What disciplines are you exercising to renew your body and mind?  4/ How is this in contrast to the pattern of the world?  5/ What are the areas of diversity among Christians?  6/ Describe the kind of attitude Paul asks for among Christians in view of these diversities.  7/ In what way is an underestimate of abilities as critical as an overestimate?  8/ List and explain the different gifts mentioned here.  9/ What function and gifts do you have?  10/ How can you show today that you are a member of *a*-the body of Christ and *b*-one another?

DAY *20*  △  *Romans 12:9-21*

1/ Categorize and explain these exhortations. What main ideas are expressed and emphasized?  2/ How are these exhortations a logical outgrowth of verses 1-2?  3/ Compare or contrast these exhortations with your present ethics.  4/ Imagine the effect of obeying them. What would be the specific results in your life? in your group? with other people?  5/ How will you obey them today?

DAY *21*  △  *Romans 13:1-7*

1/ What are your obligations to civil authorities (relate to 12:2)?

2/ Determine the meaning of *subject*. Why must a person be subject? 3/ Determine the meaning of *governing*. How does this relate to revolutions? 4/ In what ways are authorities an extension of God's authority in relation to men? 5/ When does a person have reason to fear rulers? 6/ In what specific ways do you try to "get around" your obligations? Why? What effects do these actions have on your conscience toward God? 7/ What is the basis of criminal retribution? Contrast this with contemporary popular opinion about the priority of the criminal's welfare. 8/ Imagine you are in the place of authority. As a result of understanding these principles what is your attitude toward *a*-God, *b*-your authority, *c*-those who are *subject* to you? 9/ What attitude, do you think, should a Christian have if he is being punished when he believes he is right?

### DAY 22   △   *Romans 13:8-14*

1/ How is love related to justice (cf. vv. 1-7)? to the law? 2/ In what ways does love enable you to fulfill obligations to others? 3/ Characterize this kind of *love*. If man truly loved like this, would any commandment ever be broken? Why, do you think? 4/ How will you *love your neighbor as yourself* today? In what specific ways? 5/ What is another reason for fulfilling your obligations to others? In what way does Paul picture your realization of this fact? 6/ Characterize the attitudes and actions belonging to *a-darkness* and *night* and *b-light* and *day* (cf. 6:1-10). 7/ Categorize your present ethics and behavior under these headings. 8/ What is Paul's command concerning these attitudes and actions? What is your response to that command?

### DAY 23   △   *Romans 14:1-12*

1/ Relate the necessity of Paul's words here to the cosmopolitan nature of Rome. 2/ To whom are Paul's words addressed? 3/ List the distinctions between the *strong* and the *weak* as to their opinions. 4/ How is each conscious of his indebtedness to God (cf. 12:1-2)? 4/ What are the likely attitudes of the *strong* toward the *weak*? the *weak* toward the *strong*? Why is each of these attitudes condemned? 5/ What is your attitude toward Christians with whom you differ in conviction and practice? Why? 6/ In what ways does judging others on these matters ignore *a*-the power of Christ and *b*-the final authority and place of judgment? 7/ In what ways do you recognize the lordship of Christ in your opinions, actions, and life?

DAY 24  △  *Romans 14:13-23*

1/ What substitute for *judging* does Paul command?  2/ What is the basic fallacy of the *weak's* conviction concerning abstinence (cf. vv. 1-12)? In what ways is it based on a false view of *a*-God and *b*-human responsibility?  4/ How then are the actions of a person who believes he can "eat" but abstains because of possible injury to someone who believes he can't "eat" related to love? to Christ's death?  5/ In what ways can the *good* (liberty) of the *strong* become *evil*?  6/ When questions of food and drink are a Christian's main concern, what does this reveal about his perspective as to the kingdom of God?  7/ How does Paul define *a-right* and *wrong* and *b*-sin here? Apply these to your situation.  8/ With whom must you ultimately keep your faith and life?  9/ How can you *serve* Christ and *act in faith* in similar situations today? in the future?

DAY 25  △  *Romans 15:1-13*

1/ What is to characterize Christians' relationships with each other? 2/ What are the *strong's* obligation to the *weak*?  3/ To what ends are you to *please* and *welcome* your neighbor (cf. 14:15-16)? Why? 4/ What restraints and qualifications do you place on your acceptance of other Christians? In what ways do these actions ignore Christ's example?  5/ What are the two specific things Christ's example has accomplished?  6/ What is the purpose of Old Testament scripture?  7/ What is the main emphasis of the quotations concerning the Gentiles?  8/ How are *steadfastness, encouragement,* and *hope* related to the Scriptures? to God? Can hope exist in a vacuum?  9/ What is the source of your *joy* and *peace*?

DAY 26  △  *Romans 15:14-33*

1/ What is Paul's assessment of the virtues of the Roman Christians? 2/ How does Paul picture his relationship to them (cf. 1:5; 11:13; 12:3)?  3/ Why is Paul *proud* of his work? Contrast this kind of pride with the boasting in 2:17-23 and 3:27-28.  4/ Distinguish the references to the persons of the trinity.  5/ In what ways does Christ act through the apostle? What are the results?  6/ Describe the policy of Paul's ministry as to its *a*-scope and *b*-limitation. How does he support his policy from *Isaiah*?  7/ What is the motive and purpose of the contribution of Macedonia and Achaia?  8/ In what ways do you contribute materially to those who have given you *spiritual blessings*?  9/ Describe the kind of prayer Paul requests. 10/ What is the content of your prayers for missionaries?  11/ In what situations does the God of peace give you peace?

DAY 27  △  *Romans 16:1-16*

1/ How does Paul show personal concern for the Romans?  2/ What is the place of letters and greetings in your life?  3/ List and explain the characteristics of the people Paul mentions.  4/ Imagine you are a Roman Christian. What phrase honestly characterizes you?  5/ How, do you think, does Paul know about the Christians when he has not been to Rome yet?  6/ In what ways does Paul reveal his consciousness of his connection to the church (cf. 12:4-5)? What is your relation to the church in the world? How can you express this relationship?

DAY 28  △  *Romans 16:17-27*

1/ Characterize the people Paul warns against. Why?  2/ In what ways can you be *wise* and *guileless* today?  3/ Relate God's *peace* (cf. 15:33) to a-Satan's defeat and b-Christ's *grace*.  4/ Compare this doxology (vv. 25-27) with Paul's salutation and introduction (1:1-17).  5/ How is *strength* related to the gospel?  6/ Describe the mystery of God as to a-purpose, b-authority, c-agent of disclosure, and d-scope of application.  7/ Relate God's *wisdom* to a-the mystery and b-verses 17-20.  8/ In what ways will you glorify God today?

DAY 29  △  *Romans 9—16*

1/ Summarize Paul's teaching about God's sovereignty and man's responsibility. How does this apply to Israel? to the Gentiles?  2/ Summarize how a Christian is to act toward a-God, b-the state, c-other Christians, and d-all men.  3/ How are love and obligation related?  4/ Distinguish *weakness* (chap. 14) in the contemporary world. Why can't it be gluttony or drunkenness?  5/ Summarize what is included in the *doctrine which you have been taught* (16:17).  6/ What is your doctrine? In what ways is it a part of your daily living?

DAY *30* △ *Romans 1—16*

1/ Summarize Paul's teaching of *a*-sin and righteousness, *b*-law and grace, *c*-works and faith, *d*-death and life, and *e*-flesh and spirit. 2/ What analogies and illustrations does Paul use to explain his teaching? In what ways are they appropriate? 3/ Compare or contrast your *a*-attitude toward and *b*-knowledge of the Old Testament scripture with Paul's. 4/ How have the truths of *Romans* affected your *a*-understanding of the relationship of Jews and Gentiles; *b*-understanding of God, Jesus Christ, and the Holy Spirit; *c*-understanding of yourself; and *d*-relationship with others?